CABLE TV ADVERTISING

CABLE TV ADVERTISING

In Search of the Right Formula

EDITED BY

Rajeev Batra AND Rashi Glazer

QUORUM BOOKS

New York • Westport, Connecticut • London

Library of Congress Cataloging-in-Publication Data

Cable TV advertising : in search of the right formula / edited by
  Rajeev Batra and Rashi Glazer.
      p. cm.
    Papers presented at a conference held 5/87 and co-sponsored by the
    Center for Telecommunications and Information Studies of Columbia
    University's Graduate School of Business and the firm of Coopers &
    Lybrand.
    Bibliography: p.
    Includes index.
    ISBN 0–89930–406–0 (lib. bdg. : alk. paper)
    1. Cable television advertising—United States—Congresses.
  I. Batra, Rajeev. II. Glazer, Rashi. III. Columbia University.
  Center for Telecommunications and Information Studies. IV. Coopers
  & Lybrand.
  HF6146.T42C28   1989
  659.14′3′0973—dc19   88–37395

British Library Cataloguing in Publication Data is available.

Library of Congress Catalog Card Number: 88–37395
ISBN: 0–89930–406–0

First published in 1989 by Quorum Books

Greenwood Press, Inc.
88 Post Road West, Westport, Connecticut 06881

Printed in the United States of America

The paper used in this book complies with the
Permanent Paper Standard issued by the National
Information Standards Organization (Z39.48–1984).

10 9 8 7 6 5 4 3 2 1

Contents

PART II: IMPLICATIONS FOR ADVERTISING

PART III: NEW HORIZONS

Figures and Tables

Tables

Preface

The cable television industry is now at a pivotal point in its development. While the size of the viewing audience has increased rapidly, the growth of advertising revenues—despite a recent spurt—continues to lag significantly behind early forecasts. The question that continues to confront the industry is whether cable is finally ready to fulfill its promise as perhaps the major force in the communications environment, or is destined to remain a secondary player.

In May 1987 a conference was held in New York City to explore this question. Co-sponsored by the Center for Telecommunications and Information Studies of Columbia University's Graduate School of Business and by the firm of Coopers and Lybrand, the conference brought together leading academic researchers and industry professionals to discuss the underlying factors that determine where cable TV advertising is today and what can and should be done in the future. This book represents the conclusions of the conference and includes a few chapters on related topics that were not discussed at that conference.

In the first chapter, we begin with a strategic overview of the industry's options and a review of the other chapters in this volume. The chapters in this book are organized into three parts, around the themes of industry analysis, implications for advertisers, and new developments. The first two parts are followed by the comments of industry representatives.

This book represents, to the best of our knowledge, one of the first attempts to bring together the views of academics and industry practitioners interested in the marketing and advertising implications of what one might loosely call "the new media": cable television, VCRs, videotex, etc. We believe that this volume contains a very useful exchange of ideas, and hope that it will provide new insights to those in industry and new research ideas to those engaged in the study of these new media.

We have various people to thank for making this book possible: the contributors to this volume; Eli Noam of the Center for Telecommunications and Information Studies at the Columbia Business School; Doug Conn and Rich Kramer; and Bill Battino and many others at Coopers and Lybrand. We also wish to thank the *Journal of Advertising* for permission to reproduce copyrighted figures and tables in Chapter 3, from the journal article by Roland Rust and Naveen Donthu on cable television that appeared in that journal in 1988.

Rajeev Batra
Rashi Glazer

Part I

Industry Analysis

1

Cable TV Advertising: A Strategic Overview

Rashi Glazer and Rajeev Batra

Introduction

In this introductory chapter, we present a brief overview of how to think strategically about the issues confronting cable TV advertising. The authors are both professors of marketing, and the framework presented thus reflects the traditional marketing orientation to strategic problems: a perspective whose purpose is to help decision-makers best achieve their objectives in light of customer needs, competitive pressures, and their own resource constraints. The goal is to develop a unifying structure around which the host of specific issues associated with advertising and cable TV—selection of target audiences, design of appropriate programming and advertising, methodologies for collecting ratings data, etc.—can be organized and addressed.

While the contributors to this volume represent a number of distinct perspectives on these issues, the general consensus is that cable has not in fact lived up to its original promise and that system operators, programmers as well as advertisers, are collectively guilty of a myopic view towards the medium, which has resulted in the delayed growth. More specifically, despite almost two decades of lip-service to the idea that cable TV is indeed a fundamentally new and unique medium, the repeated decisions of all players involved suggest that the industry still *acts* as if it were an alternative to—and therefore competes with—traditional mass-audience broadcast television.

This inconsistency between attitudes and behaviors has been responsible for both the initially optimistic forecasts and the subsequently disappointing results. It is now clear that if the industry is to realize its promise—and this remins the most likely scenario—it will happen only in light of a fundamental reassessment of its strategic position within the overall communications and information-technology environment. Such a strategic reassessment can provide a framework within which operational and tactical marketing decisions can then be made.

In what follows, we begin by illustrating what the conclusions of a typical strategic situation analysis of the cable industry might reveal, where the situation analysis (which we do not present in detail) represents a systematic investigation into the consumer, competitive, product-specific and general environmental factors that guide decision-makers in formulating a particular strategic direction. We then describe how the remaining chapters in the book develop in greater detail the general themes and issues raised in this introduction. Finally, we present an outline of possible directions for future research.

It should be noted that the primary purpose of this book is to stimulate (or, in some cases, revitalize), on one hand, a formal interest by academics in the practical concerns posed by the introduction of the new cable technology and, on the other, an appreciation by industry practitioners of the theoretical contributions that the academic community can make to the industry. It is a curious, yet perhaps not coincidental development that, in an arena that has produced results far short of everyone's expectations, the degree of contact between industry and academics and the level of academic research have been disappointing given the importance of the problem. If this book can help to rectify this state of affairs, we will have accomplished our objective.

A Strategic Perspective

The history of media reveals that the form of the old becomes the content of the new; or that new technology and hardware are programmed with old software. Thus in this century, for example, the content of movies and radio has been theatre; the content of television, movies and radio. Often, it is not until relatively late in a medium's evolution—indeed, sometimes not until the emergence of an even newer technology—that it develops its own identity and displays the characteristics that make it unique. Typically this is so because, in the early stages of a medium's life cycle, everyone concerned tends to focus on the technology/hardware at the expense of the programming and software. Such has been the case with cable TV.

It is therefore not surprising that the content of cable TV has been broadcast television. At the same time, it is also not surprising that, in the absence of a unique identity, cable competes economically with broadcast. However, unlike, say, the differences between theatre and film, the distinctions between cable and broadcast television are easier to ignore; the two media *can* be considered, at least superficially, technologically equivalent. As a result, to the extent that the organization and content of cable programming mirrors that of the older broadcast form, the newer medium is bound to be at a competitive disadvantage. Whatever cable does, broadcast has been doing better and for a much longer time! Even if they have been unaware of the underlying causes, this fact has not been lost on advertisers as they have been making their media purchase decisions.

The strategic marketing perspective we present here recognizes that marketplace success reflects the interaction among three factors:

1. The differential advantages of the product or service being offered
2. The needs of a particular target group, or groups, of consumers for whom the advantages of the offering represent real benefits
3. The alternative offerings of an *appropriately defined* group of competitors

In effect, a good strategy represents the outcome of a situation analysis designed to ascertain: what is really being offered; who really wants what is being offered; and who else is really offering the same thing?

In the case of cable TV advertising, it is important to realize that there are two generic groups of consumers: program viewers and advertisers. As a result, there are also, in effect, two products: the programming/advertising, delivered to the program viewers; and the viewers themselves, who constitute the product for the advertisers, in the sense that the cable operator delivers an audience of viewers to the advertisers.

Product

There are essentially two dimensions which must be considered in assessing the differential advantages of cable TV as a communications medium: the *video* dimension, which cable shares with other technologies such as broadcast and videocassette, but which distinguishes it from other media such as print and radio; and the *cable* dimension, which is not shared by other video-based technologies.

The most salient attribute of video, of course, is the ability to convey simultaneously both moving-image and audio information, thus distinguishing the medium from print and radio. If desired, information can be transmitted in "real-time" (i.e., live) or, via tape, immediately after recording. It is this "real-time" feature that technically distinguishes video from film, since both communicate audio visual information.

With regard to the social, as opposed to technological, viewing environment, video tends to be seen at home—often privately—and film in public theatres; though, as noted, a good deal of the content of television programming is film. (Some media theorists and artists also call attention to the aesthetic concerns associated with the "texture" or "feel" of electronic-based videotape as opposed to chemical-based film. These issues are beyond the scope of the current discussion.)

A sometimes negative attribute of video—which it shares with other "continuous" audio and audio visual media, but *not* with the printed page—is the inability to control the pace and sequence of the information presented. (To the extent that video technology acts merely as an electronic storage for printed material, with random access capabilities, this difference is negated.)

In contrast to other video media (broadcast television in particular), cable's distinguishing attributes are a dramatic increase in overall channel capacity and two-way communications capability. The first feature serves to move television away from being a mass or centralized information vehicle towards being a more personal and decentralized one. (Videocassette technology represents, of course, the extreme case of individualized program delivery, though only with respect to pre-recorded material.) The second feature introduces the possibility of truly interactive or bi-directional audio-visual communication, thereby replacing the typical patterns—of linear information flow and passive audiences—with feedback loops that allow active audience participation.

The differential advantage of cable TV, then, when compared with other communications media, is this: once relieved of the necessity to satisfy the needs of a relatively homogeneous audience, television programmers are free to provide dramatically greater levels of variety in both program content as well as format (e.g., length); therefore, programming decisions can be made within a substantially reduced regulatory environment.

The social implications of the so-called "wired nation" and the "television of abundance" (as opposed to the older broadcast-induced "television of scarcity"), resulting from significant penetration of cable networks free of technological and regulatory constraints, have been understood for several decades. However, what has apparently not been as well understood are the strategic implications of the inherent differential advantages of the cable TV medium, particularly as they impact the generation of advertising revenues.

In particular, it is becoming apparent that the defining characteristic of cable is what has come to be called "narrowcasting:" the delivery of specialized programming to specific interest groups—which implies the delivery of these specific target audiences to specialized advertisers. At the same time, it should be clear that the appropriately defined *competitive* group for cable is not broadcast television, but those media whose strategic focus is also narrow target markets. This group, of course, is largely concentrated in the print media—notably, specialty magazines—a development which fortuitously allows cable to capitalize on those differentiating attributes associated with video media in general. The appropriate positioning of cable TV as such a specialized medium is discussed later.

The strategic challenge facing the industry is thus how to create a climate in which cable TV is looked to by both audiences and advertisers as *the* medium for specialized targeted communications. In industry after industry (largely as a result of the explosion in telecommunications and data processing), the homogeneous mass market is giving way to smaller fragmented submarkets characterized by heterogeneous consumer preferences. Indeed, the tremendous success of targeted media such as specialty magazines (and, more recently, direct mail and radio) is evidence of the growing trend towards segmented communications markets, but it also indicates that both consumers and advertisers look to media other than cable for the satisfaction of their specialized information needs.

Consumers

The fact is that, today, individuals expect cable television to provide what broadcast television provides; they look to other media instead for those benefits that cable should provide. This suggests that the real strategic task facing the industry is one of consumer education, or *investment in market development*. This is radically different from investing in the technological infrastructure, or even in programming as such, particularly if the progamming is intended to attract the largest possible audience and is therefore essentially familiar to the viewers.

While a fair amount of theoretical work has been done—by communications scholars, sociologists, and other academics—concerning the diffusion of cable television (and other media) throughout society, there is little evidence that these studies have played any formal role in the strategic marketing decisions of the industry. Instead, the industry seems largely to have followed the path of least resistance: by positioning cable television as simply an extension of broadcast television it has obtained short-term returns from those who were most accepting of such a positioning. The "long-term" challenge—more difficult initially, but probably more profitable eventually—of finding those consumers desiring specialized video programming seems to have been ignored.

Perhaps the major implication of the preceding discussion is that the cable industry as a whole must become dramatically more marketing research–intensive, though with an orientation somewhat different than typical audience-measurement exercises. The focus on size of audience alone should be abandoned in favor of concerns with the potential depth of interest generated by particular program offerings.

Such an approach, ironically, represents a return to the issue that initially dominated the public discussion over cable TV, and that has since been relatively ignored: the availability of local access or community-oriented programming. The failure of the cable industry to develop significant levels of local-origination programming (supported by local advertising) would be seen more as a curious phenomenon than as a serious manifestation of the industry's strategic misdirection, were it not for the fact that, during the same period, community and regional print media have been booming!

There are, of course, some notable examples of specialized targeted programming (MTV, Nickelodeon, ESPN), but they are the exception rather than the rule in the overall cable schedule; and even these channels define their audiences in broad terms, despite the emphasis on specialized programming. Indeed, beyond a few obvious candidates (news, sports, rock videos), the real lesson of the content-dedicated networks may be that segmentation by channel is less desirable than segmentation by programming, or programming-audience interface.

The discussion so far has placed responsibility for development of the appropriate strategic direction for the industry on the cable system operators. However, it would appear that the advertising community, too, must take more responsibility than it has for the creation of a healthy cable viewing environment. Although, as noted, advertisers are, in one capacity, the cable industry's customers, they also gain if cable television develops as a major marketing medium, thereby reducing the negotiating clout of the broadcast television networks.

The situation in cable today reflects the chicken-and-egg paradigm with respect to advertising and programming, or advertisers and audience. Until there is a sufficient audience, advertisers wait; but until there is sufficient advertising, there is not enough programming to build the audience, and so on. While such a model may have been relevant for the mass-market-oriented broadcast environment, it may not apply to cable, since it ignores the differential advantages of the new medium.

The constraints associated with mass-market–oriented broadcasting limit the amount of detailed information that can be communicated about products advertised, so that the content of broadcast television advertising is typically subsidiary to stylistic or format issues. It has also become increasingly difficult for a given advertiser to match a particular ad to the editorial context (i.e., programming) in which it is embedded. By contrast, the greater freedom afforded the advertiser in the cable environment opens up a world of creative possibilities and flexibility with respect to both content and format.

Perhaps the most significant consequence of this expanded flexibility is the ability to communicate substantially more information about the product. Furthermore, the opportunity exists to develop and display advertising that is appropriate for specific editorial climates. As a result, the information content of commercial messages assumes renewed importance, until the advertising itself becomes a form of programming.

One of the most dramatic implications of the idea of cable TV narrowcasting is that the boundary between editorial or programming material and advertising begins to dissolve. However, this notion challenges the assumption that the audience for programming must be in place prior to advertiser participation. On the contrary, perhaps advertising—properly designed as *information*—should be used to create the audience in the first place, under the premise that people will watch a particular program as much for the advertising they expect to find there as for the editorial content.

Competition

We mentioned earlier that a strategic analysis of cable television as an advertising medium must necessarily give prominence to the ways in which it can distinguish itself from competing advertising media. Some of these advantages have already been mentioned: the interactive, audiovisual nature of the medium, the reduced degree of regulation, and the ability to tailor advertising to the editorial content. Yet clearly the most distinguishing feature of cable TV as an advertising medium—the capability to narrowcast to specialized audiences—is an area in which it has clearly failed to establish itself.

In our opinion, the crucial question facing cable television advertising is this: how should it position itself as an advertising medium? It seems fair to say that the dominant thrust thus far has been to position it as an alternative to network television. This effort has been only partly successful. We think there are at least two reasons for this failure.

First, big advertisers and their advertising agencies have always used network television for mass reach. By positioning itself as an alternative to network television, cable television has found itself judged with network television's criteria of mass reach and low cost-per-thousand. With only 60% household penetration, and extremely small individual channel ratings, cable TV has failed to deliver on such a perceived promise.

Second, in trying to acquire mass reach, cable has either tried to out-network the networks, with mass and undistinguished programming—and failed to generate large audiences—or has, with some exceptions, offered specialized programming on a 24-hour basis to audiences that are only willing to view a few hours of it. (The exceptions, of course, are channels like MTV, ESPN, etc.) One wonders whether the strategy of segmenting by special interest channels is too ambitious. Viewers do read and view specialized material, such as most magazines, but most of their hours are spent on general-interest pursuits.

A way to please both advertisers and viewers may suggest itself from the following analysis. Advertisers *do* use specialized media, such as magazines and direct mail, and perhaps cable should position itself against them, rather than against network television. The question then will not be whether cable can deliver mass audiences on an efficient cost-per-thousand basis, as network television can, but rather how cable can reach specialized audiences more effectively than magazines and direct mail.

Clearly, cable will score higher here on its audiovisual capabilities; but it is not currently positioned as geographically targetable in comparison with direct mail and the geographic editions of many magazines. This is where cable perhaps should innovate. For example, it can develop a time-selling framework that lets advertisers buy cable not only on a special channel basis, but also on a local cable system basis. It might be useful to enable advertisers to buy certain cable households by zip code and census block group, much like direct mail names are rented. It could then be a viable competitor to magazines and direct mail, and to local and spot, if not network, television.

In order to be able to offer such advertising opportunities, of course, cable television must first attract local audiences. This is the programming side of the fence. Amazingly, most cable systems have not attempted to develop their own local programming, in the manner of newspapers. It would be interesting to see if, for example, New York cable systems could offer programming (their own, or syndicated) aimed at young Yuppie parents living on the upper west side of Manhattan, and then sell advertising time to advertisers who have no other audiovisual means of reaching these specific consumers. For this to happen, of course, the multiple system operators must take a far more active role in the creation and selling of advertising time. A recent news item (*New York Times*, September 5, 1988) suggests that this may have begun to occur: the dominant system on Long Island in New York has now started a 24-hour regional broadcast of Long Island news reaching 540,000 homes in Nassau and Suffolk counties. Apparently it is watched at least once a day by 42% of Long Island's cable households, outranking Home Box Office (HBO) and several independent New York City stations. More such local programming is obviously required.

The Chapters

The individual chapters in this book can be organized with respect to the overall perspective just presented. In "Cable Television Advertising: Is the Promise Being Fulfilled?" William Battino and James DePalma, both of Coopers and Lybrand, expand upon the strategic framework and situation analysis presented in this introduction. In particular, based upon a series of in-depth personal interviews with cable TV system operators, programmers, advertising agencies and advertisers, they discuss the implications for cable of general media trends towards narrowcasting, regionalization and direct marketing. As part of their analysis, they also provide an economic overview of cable advertising revenues.

To the extent that targeted programming is the appropriate strategic direction for cable to take, the next chapter, "Programming Holes: Opportunities for Cable Networks," by Professors Roland Rust and Naveen Donthu, presents a methodology by which the positioning of potential cable networks can be achieved. The chapter describes the application of the increasingly popular marketing research technique of multidimensional scaling to map the perceptual space of the cable viewing audience relative to broadcast networks. The result is a picture of the marketplace in which a given cable channel can identify a unique market niche that maximizes either audience size or revenue potential. Chapter 4 presents comments by two industry practitioners, based on the premise that narrowcasting is the appropriate methodology, and comments on some strengths and weaknesses of the model.

We then move to Part II of the book: Implications for Advertising. The fifth chapter, "The Television Viewing Environment: Implications of Audience Change," by Professor Dean Krugman, explores the theme that knowledge of the consumer decision-making process, particularly an appreciation of how innovations are adopted, is crucial to marketplace success. The chapter reviews a number of research studies which place cable in the broader context of the appearance of new video technologies and the attendant shifts that are emerging in viewing habits. Among the important implications for the cable industry, and cable advertisers in particular, is an understanding not just of who watches cable, but of how they watch cable, and therefore of how cable can weave itself into local-oriented/targeted viewing patterns.

Continuing the exploration of issues raised by cable concerning consumer analyis, the sixth chapter, "Collecting Ratings Data for Cable Channels," by Professor Seymour Sudman, discusses the all-important question of audience measurement, on which most advertising decisions are based. In keeping with the strategic theme developed, the implication here is that high ratings as such may be misleading, in that they divert attention from *who* is watching to *how many*. The chapter reviews a number of different methodological alternatives for collecting ratings data for low-rated cable channels and presents a forecast of methods that might be used in the future. One important point that comes out (which, ironically, is also emerging with respect to the people meter issue for broadcast television) is that active-interview-based data should not be expected to match the numbers obtained from typical diary panels, where the response bias tends to overrate popular shows. This may be one reason why cable has not succeeded in siphoning off advertising dollars from the broadcast networks. In chapter 8 three industry practitioners comment on the viewer habit and ratings methodology issues raised in chapters 5 and 6.

Turning to the perspective of advertising effectiveness, the seventh chapter, by Professor Rajeev Batra, discusses some hypotheses on how cable television advertisers can more closely tailor their ads to the nature of the program context.

These two sets of chapters in the book focus on cable's role as a provider of traditional one-way advertiser-supported television programming. However, no volume on the future of cable communications would be complete without a discussion of some of those more novel services associated with the medium which call attention to its unique capabilities. The last section in the book deals with two of these services.

Chapter 9, "In-Home Shopping: Impact of Television Shopping Programs," by Professor Wayne Talarzyk, compares the issues surrounding the phenomenon of in-home shopping in cable, broadcast and videotex media. In-home shopping, perhaps more than any other development, represents the extreme case of product advertising and programming merging into a single form. Focusing on those aspects of electronic retailing that facilitate the steps in the consumer shopping process, the paper discusses both what has been learned so far about television shopping programs as well as future scenarios for the industry and the strategies for dealing with them. In chapter 10, DongHoon Kim (a doctoral student at Columbia) presents a mathematical analysis of how long a product on such in-home shopping services should be on the air to maximize the probability that a viewer might buy it, but not be bored enough to switch channels.

The final chapter, "The Pay-per-View Experience: Insights from a Field Experiment," by Professors Dean Krugman and Terry Childers, treats another aspect of interactive cable television technology: pay-per-view programming. To the extent that pay-per-view becomes a dominant form of cable programming, the implications for advertising are obvious, particularly if advertising is excluded from pay-per-view networks. The chapter first presents a conceptual framework for understanding how groups of consumers differ with respect to their propensity to adopt a new service like pay-per-view; and then it presents the results of a field experiment designed to elicit consumer reactions to the innovative technology.

As mentioned, following most chapters are the comments of a number of distinguished industry professionals whose experience enables them to evaluate the relevance of conceptual or theoretical issues to the practical aspects of the areas under study. We found these comments to be extremely provocative, and hope that you will too.

When taken as a group, the chapters in this volume suggest the range of topics that are appropriate subjects for research aimed at a general understanding of cable television advertising. In concluding this chapter, we present the outline of a research agenda based on the strategic orientation presented in this introduction. It should be noted that the areas suggested supplement specific research agendas that are part of several of the chapters in the book.

1. The advent of a new medium like cable television, and therefore of an associated new type of advertising, calls attention more than anything else to the need for research on the form of media, and media advertising itself, and not just on the content of particular progams or ads. The goal is to develop a precise understanding of those properties which distinguish one medium—for example, cable advertising—from others, and to develop testable hypotheses about the effects of the medium on human behavior—particularly consumer behavior.

We should emphasize that the focus here is on research conducted by individuals—typically business school academics in departments of marketing and advertising—who are interested in the commercial application of their work to the practical problems of the cable industry. We emphasize this point because some of the research needed echoes research done by persons in other disciplines. Perhaps because the academic disciplines of marketing and advertising matured after most traditional media networks were already in place, scholars in these fields never developed the habit of studying the formal properties of the media as such. This is in contrast to their counterparts in communications theory, sociology, and related areas, who have addressed some of these issues but have ignored their commercial import, most notably the advertising implications.

2. In a related vein, the study of how commercial media—for instance, cable advertising—diffuses through a society should become a research priority. The more general area of the diffusion of innovations has been well-developed, but the focus (as noted above) tends to be on technology or hardware. What is required is a better understanding of how software—codified types of information or programming—gets adapted by a culture, with respect to the timing as well as the patterns of adoption. Of particular interest is the extent to which the prior research is relevant to the new domain, or if information/software products and services have different characteristics with respect to the diffusion process than have been observed with more traditional technologies.

3. Since both operators and advertisers have seen cable as an alternative to broadcast television, they have also assumed that consumer behavior towards the new medium is the same as towards the old. As a result, little is known about how individual viewers actually behave with respect to cable. A research stream that focused on an understanding of the decision-making process regarding cable would help both operators/programmers as well as advertisers to respond to market needs.

Among specific research questions to be addressed are: what role do individuals see cable playing in their overall communication activities? How do individuals decide to watch a cable program? What criteria do they use? How do families deal with the multi-person decision-making issue in regard to cable viewing? Who in the family influences the viewing process?

4. Assuming that the strategic goal of cable advertising is narrowcasting, research is needed in how to collect better data where audience size is not the primary criterion. On one hand, techniques need to be developed that are accurate—that is, the measures produced are reliable and valid—in the absence of large sample sizes. At the same time, methodologies must be discovered that produce information about market quality, as opposed to quantity. As noted above, this is becoming a major concern of marketing in almost all product categories, but the particular strategic requirements of the cable industry make it crucial to the industry's long-term survival.

5. Indeed, in general, research is needed on how to develop measures which accurately reflect the investment in long-term audience building—in the creation of what the marketing community calls the establishment of a "consumer franchise"—upon which most successful cable strategies will depend. In the final analysis—and this is something that cable TV shares increasingly with other industries in the information economy—the ability to place a value on an individual viewer and to see that viewer as the firm's primary asset will differentiate the leaders in the industry from the rest of the system operators.

We look forward to development of this and other research, and are pleased to have facilitated the presentation of the analysis and recommendations contained in this volume.

2

Cable Television Advertising: Is the Promise Being Fulfilled?

William Battino and James DePalma

Introduction

The promise of cable television has always been the delivery of diverse and innovative programming to three main beneficiaries: subscribers, who enjoy more entertainment and information with cable than without it; advertising agencies, which expand the media with which they do business; and advertisers, who gain a new outlet for their advertising. This chapter focuses on cable's promise solely from an advertising perspective.

Advertising on cable television comprises commercial insertions on national and local broadcasts. National advertising time is principally offered through basic programming services, and local advertising by cable systems. Both kinds of outlets face challenges in adapting to, and expanding, the advertising they carry. For basic programmers who seek advertising, the challenge lies in continually balancing the interests of the cable subscriber and the advertiser. For many local cable operators, generating advertising requires a new way of thinking, because advertising revenues represent a largely untapped but potentially lucrative source of funds. We examine how successful both have been in meeting the promise that cable television offers to advertisers and agencies.

The report on which this chapter is based relied on personal interviews with advertising agencies, advertisers, multiple system operators (MSOs) and cable programmers. These interviews were conducted to gain greater understanding of their attitudes toward national and local advertising on cable. Respondent feedback and analysis of basic programmers will be covered first, followed by a discussion of local advertising.

Basic Programming

It should be noted at the outset that cable television is moving quickly toward a more mature—and financially rewarding—phase in its evolution. At the system (MSO) level, growth in the industry has been dominated by acquisitions. Aggressive purchasers such as TCI have grown dramatically, to Wall Street's applause. Investors have recognized that, as in other communications businesses, cash flows, subscribers, and margins are valid criteria for analyzing cable companies. Rewards are given to more efficient companies that purchase a system and increase profitability through implementation of proven management practices. Deregulation of basic cable has also led to increased success as operators raised rates and customers paid readily. Not too long ago, one of the ten largest systems increased basic rates from $10.75 to $14.50, with less than one-tenth of 1% of its subscribers being churned, or lost.

For basic programmers, however, such maturity does not necessarily mean continued success. While basic programmers have been able to flex their muscles and demand higher subscriber fees (proportionate to higher basic rates) from the systems, their task in raising advertising revenues is more difficult. Their challenge lies in translating their success in building household viewership to success in attaining agency and advertiser support.

A key element in this challenge is the resolution of an identity crisis, which seems to be growing among basic programmers and the agencies and advertisers. Four basic questions need resolution:

1. Who really is the competition for basic programming?
2. What is the appropriate positioning for cable television advertising?
3. What are programmers' stances on narrowcasting and regionalization?
4. Finally, just how should basic programmers be pricing and selling advertising time?

Below, we examine each of these issues in turn.

Competition

To determine "who is the competition for basic programmers?" we put that question, simply and directly, to the executives interviewed. Four different perspectives emerged:

1. "Cable will always be a secondary programming supplier. Fellow basic programmers are the real competition." Given cable's original promise, this seemed a fairly narrow definition of who basic programmers are and with whom they compete. Surprisingly, this answer was given by some of the basic programmers themselves.
2. "Basic programmers compete among themselves for agency dollars and for eyeballs with the networks." This slight variation of the first theme

was the most common viewpoint. It underscores the fairly obvious observation that basic programmers' ratings do not just compete with each other, but have to be compared with those of networks, affiliates and independents. However, the more subtle and meaningful point made here was that, despite this comparison, agencies do view cable television quite differently than they view networks. Agencies place about 4% of their client's dollars behind cable right now, *but only 4%*. The programmers' challenge is to compete for their share of that 4%, showing why they offer a better way of spending *cable* dollars.

3. "Cable programmers must stop behaving like radio stations and promote the medium more than the service. They compete as a medium." Radio, which consists of many stations in a given market, typically experiences a high degree of infighting among stations. Basic programmers, it was argued, would be smart to avoid this infighting and concentrate first on increasing cable's share of media advertising plans from 4% to 10–15%. Then they could focus on their proportion of those shares. This strategy would try to increase the overall amount of cable advertising buys and thereby promote the medium—not just each particular programming service.

   This opinion thus holds that cable television is not getting its fair share of advertising dollars. A recent Nielsen Television Index (NTI) Cable TV Status Report showed that basic cable television attracts 14% viewership among all television households and 24% viewership among cable households. Admittedly, these ratings must be adjusted to reflect that cable is subscribed to by approximately 50% of American households. If viewership ratings are reduced by half to reflect this fact, to 7% in all American households, the 4% of advertising dollars spent on cable clearly does not parallel viewership. This disparity is even more exaggerated when the upscale demographic profile of cable viewers is considered. Cable advertising placement should almost double to reflect levels of viewership.

4. "Cable must reckon with VCRs, which are here to stay; we have to make the best of it." This was a fairly universal view of the VCR and emerging technologies, reflecting the recognition that VCR penetration today is just about outstripping cable penetration.

   However, VCRs must be viewed as a complement rather than as a competitor to cable. Agencies, advertisers and cable respondents seem to have learned a lesson that pay programmers taught the motion picture industry. Initially, theatre chains protested the new competitive threat to pay TV; but at the same time they were experiencing some of the best box office years in history. Originally perceived as a threat, HBO ultimately increased the demand for entertainment products. Distributors' demand for exhibition screens rose. Similarly, cable programmers first feared VCRs and now believe they can stimulate television viewing.

These varied views illustrate the industry confusion about who cable television competes with for advertising dollars—and this confusion leads to positioning problems.

Positioning

We asked both basic programmers and agencies what it was that cable television was selling.

Most often, respondents felt that cable advertising was being sold as a solution to the problem of eroding network viewership. Agencies believed the networks no longer attracted the entire television audience, resulting in underdelivery of viewers to advertisers. Cable time is thus sold as a complementary vehicle to reach the total television audience.

Such underdelivery has resulted since competitors have emerged offering alternatives to major network viewing. Networks no longer deliver 100% viewer shares. An agency professional said, "I buy cable TV time as an insurance policy." Professionals believe the networks are getting maybe 60% to 70% share, and the agencies need to reach the other 40% to 30%. There was not a clear sense of exactly where the eyeballs were straying to, but a need was perceived for a more complete blanketing of television alternatives.

Cable was identified as a leading cause of network share decline. As such, advertising dollars have been expended on basic programming services to combat the underdelivery of viewers to the advertisers.

The strategy we most often heard to accomplish this objective is what people are calling "roadblocking"—that is, buying particular time slots or dayparts across cable networks. An example would be the purchase of an 8:01 P.M. time slot across the six major cable networks. The assumption is that if someone is watching cable, the commercial will be seen on one channel or the other. There is less concern about which particular service is watched. Roadblocking strategies implicitly view cable as a homogeneous collection of services.

A different ad positioning view, and one closer to the original promise of cable, sees cable as a vehicle for delivery of purer, higher-quality demographics than network television. The CableOne venture, originated by an ad agency, is a good example. CableOne tries to position the advertising buy demographically, considering each cable service as a different delivery vehicle. For instance, if a buyer seeks a certain female demographic profile, it might purchase a combination of particular shows on CBN, Lifetime or USA, as opposed to buying a daypart. (Cable has often been cited as the video medium most targeted to reach working women.)

This media plan recognizes the special attraction of particular services and shows on cable television. In this respect, cable is seen as more closely resembling magazines than other television-based media.

It becomes clear that basic programmers have not conveyed a clear image to advertisers or agencies. Do they represent a way to combat the underdelivery of the eroding network television share? Or, do they deliver a

Figure 2.1
Categories of Service

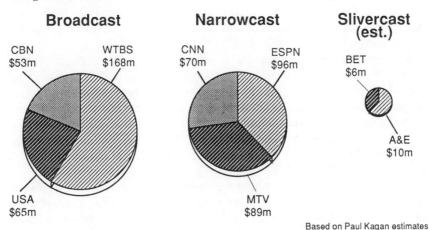

Based on Paul Kagan estimates

differentiated set of viewers? Resolution of this image problem is critical to future advertising growth of basic programming services.

Services Provided

The services offered by basic programmers can be divided into three categories: broadcast, narrowcast and slivercast, based on the homogeneity of programming within a service. As can be seen in figure 2.1, different programmers fall within these three categories.

The broadcast group (WTBS, USA, and CBN) closely resembles independent television stations, offering a wide variety of programming. Typically, this programming is dominated by syndicated shows. Original programming usually consists of newscasts, variety shows, and local sports (with superstation sports going out on a national basis).

Narrowcasters center their service around a particular theme, such as news (CNN), sports (ESPN), or music (MTV). Narrowcast services tend to attract a fairly well-defined demographic group of viewers. For example, MTV's audience skews heavily to the 12–34 age group (88%) with many of these 18–34-year-olds (57%). Both groups represent a predominantly metropolitan audience (82% in urban "A" and "B" counties, the most populated sectors).

Slivercasters attract the most homogeneous group of viewers. Their services can be thought of as niche narrowcasters. Examples of these are A&E and BET.

The six largest basic cable networks, defined by both ad revenues and subscribership, are evenly split between broadcast and narrowcast services, with TBS the largest single service. This dichotomy underlines some of the positioning confusion. When buying cable, is the advertiser simply employing another independent outlet or is it buying a different type of viewership?

Basic programmers themselves seem unclear about which way their services will evolve. Narrowcast services likely will have a clearer image and position in the long run. Clarity of image and delivery will certainly help attract advertising dollars. As for broadcast services, the recent shakeout of numerous independent stations suggests a tougher period ahead, in which program suppliers face an increasingly difficult task of differentiation. The rule of "the first one in wins" may still hold, but a relatively high attrition rate is also likely.

The slivercasters must address another fundamental question: should they attempt to attract revenues from advertising support or from affiliate fees? All cable services face the issue of substantiating significant audience share size; and for the slivercaster this problem is compounded. Currently, slivercasters aren't attracting large enough shares to attract many agency dollars, and they will not do so in the foreseeable future. Yet slivercast services can be a valuable part of the basic cable package. They tend to attract the hard-to-sign cable customer and, therefore, are quite valuable to the local system operator. The slivercasters may have to position themselves as a complementary service offering to the subscriber, filling out the basic package. If this occurs, attraction of affiliate fees becomes the primary revenue objective for them.

Regional Networks

Great hopes were placed on regional programming in the early eighties. To date, however, the notion has not lived up to initial expectations. Many of these networks were formed after the success of regional magazines. Adopting narrowcast niche marketing techniques, regional networks sought to attract like communities of interest. Unfortunately, a number of pricing and selling problems have curtailed growth—and often led to failure. In 1985, a number of notable companies, such as Spectrum of Minneapolis, SportsVue Cable Network and Sports Time went out of business. But regional networks do have a future if they address certain issues.

Regional broadcasters have been uncertain whether to position the product on pay or on basic. Our research shows that these services should be positioned on basic even though many started out on pay. MSG, the largest regional programming service, is a good example. MSG was initially offered as a pay service but now has shifted most of its subscribers to basic. Likewise, SportsVision in Chicago has shifted all of its subscribers to basic. SportsChannel recently shifted over to basic in New England. Each of

st local advertisers are familiar with newspaper, local television, ra-
nd yellow page offerings, and are less acquainted with cable televi-
Very often cable is perceived as a source of movies and sports, but
is little recognition of specific stations and viewer groups. The cable
manager must increase awareness of cable attributes. An effective
technique is marketing to specific product/service categories (e.g.,
, car dealers). Frequently, the presence of one company on cable
tract its competitors to the medium.

An Extreme Case

ew respondents felt that local cable advertising growth could take a
um leap with the support of the major networks. They believed local
systems could supplant the role of the local affiliate. Two incentives
networks to consider new distribution partners were cited:

1. Affiliate compensation. In aggregate, the networks now pay approximately $500 million a year to affiliates to carry programming. This is
   in contrast to independent television stations, which have to pay for
   programming at ever increasing rates.
2. Programming preemption. Tension between networks and affiliates
   over preemption of network broadcast is at an all-time high. Affiliates
   have increasingly substituted original programming, for which they can
   insert their own advertising, for late-night and late-morning shows.

spondents felt that if cable penetration could rise from its current
of approximately 50% to 65%, it would be viewed as a "mass market"
bution alternative. In some markets—most likely not the largest cit-
he cable operators or a consortium of operators could be strong
etition for local affiliates.
instance, a Phoenix cable system could become the local distribution
in network programming, replacing the current practice of rebroad-
g affiliate feeds. A contract could be structured to meet the needs of
ble operator and the network. The cable operator most likely would
number of valuable advertising slots, and the network could receive
nce of programming carriage and the elimination of compensation
ents. Implementation of this type of arrangement would be techno-
lly simple because most networks are now broadcasting via satellite.
ure 2.3 depicts the current distribution system and the "extreme case"
iscussed.

Interconnects

ether cable becomes a network program distributor or not, inter-
cts are crucial to the success of local advertising sales efforts. While

these regional networks is facing the problem that confronted pay programmers: justification of a premium charge.

The problems that pay networks are having in proving their price/value
relationship are well-documented. If the pay networks are having trouble
justifying an $8–$10 fee per month, most having 24-hour programming,
original production, and significant investment, it is hard to imagine sports
networks showing seven or less major live sports events a week attracting
that same type of value perception.

Regional broadcasters would be wise to focus more on advertiser support
and affiliate fees and less on direct subscriber charges. It would allow all
parties to benefit, as system operators strengthen the portfolio of basic
services, advertisers find an outlet for targeted geographic marketing with
larger reach, and consumers' price perception of cable service improves.

Market Research

Programmers, agencies, and advertisers face a number of market research hurdles. Quantitative data on cable viewership and demographics
are difficult to use, especially for agencies. Each of the 15 major basic
cable programming services provides the agencies with reports of varying
timeliness, daypart division and reporting by show. The inconsistencies
have caused confusion at the agencies, often creating a bias against younger
audiences. MTV has already conducted significant customized research,
including special Nielsen phone surveys.

Ratings interpretation is another problem. The confusion stems from
trying to integrate the different information resources that advertisers and
agencies must use to purchase time. To buy cable, they must combine the
1,700 household Nielsen Television Index meter samples, National Station
Index sweeps and National Audience Composition diary reports. It is a
logical nightmare to find a quantitative justification for buying cable time.
The upcoming increased sample size of people-meter surveys is eagerly
awaited. It is in the cable programmers' best interest to hasten the process
of generating more simplified, quantified, and integrated market research.

Packaging

The basic programmer must decide whether to market to agencies or go
directly to advertisers. If programmers feel there is an agency bias against
cable, then marketing directly to the advertiser should be considered. Many
feel agencies view cable as a time-consuming, difficult buy and, therefore,
de-emphasize it in their media plans. Marketing to the advertiser may be
one way to combat this problem.

Cable time is sold by programmers by show and in packages of shows.
Bundling or unbundling sales will emerge as a critical topic. It is a debate

which some people are calling "run-of-system" versus "fixed-position" selling.

The consensus is that run-of-system—or bundled sales—is fine for a service like MTV, which has slightly less differentiated programming throughout the day. Programmers like MSG or ESPN, which clearly have certain shows with higher profiles and interest, cannot continue to bundle sales in the future. Frequently, MSG purchasers want to buy time on the New York teams, the Knicks and Rangers, but are forced to buy a mixed package of programming that often includes older syndicated shows. This is equivalent to asking an advertiser who wants to have a commercial placed during the Super Bowl to buy a bundled package of network times across dayparts, weeks and even months. If programmers like MSG and ESPN are going to become mature and independent advertising vehicles, they must prove the merit of each individual program.

Pricing

Basic programmers initially hoped to sell advertising time at premium rates per viewer. The more targeted, upscale cable audience was thought to be a prime deliverable to the agencies. This more affluent audience and its higher-than-average spending was seen as the answer to advertisers' prayers.

While reports from Mediamark Research Inc., the market research firm, confirm the higher-grade demographics on cable, advertising time continues to sell at a discounted rate or, in advertising jargon, "cost per thousand minus (CPM −)". Many of the people interviewed cited the lack of reliable, quantitative reporting about cable television as the prime hurdle confronting programmers, though help seems on the way. A. C. Nielsen's new Cable Audience Profile is the first recognized market research analysis to provide demographic information on a system-by-system basis. Those we interviewed questioned the report's timeliness and sampling technique, but generally applauded the effort and were optimistic about future refinements.

If cable programmers are going to become more than just secondary suppliers, they must improve on selling at CPM − and try to come nearer to parity with the stronger competitors. Programmers have to resist the temptation to market services at discounted rates in the short run if they are to break the "cheap channel" perception.

Local Advertising

Another recent study by Coopers and Lybrand, *Fine Tuning Cable Television*, identified local cable advertising as a leading source of revenue growth at the system level. In the opinion of 100 cable system managers,

Figure 2.2
1986 Advertising Revenues

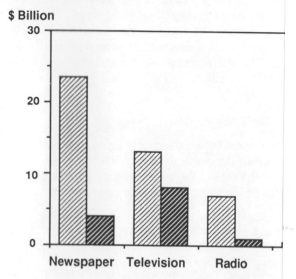

there are almost no more home runs to hit. They
singles and doubles game where advances come fr
ments to current activities. Cable advertising an
ming were the only areas considered legitimate

Local cable advertising is potentially the largest
for the MSO. For cable's competitors, local adver
prevalent than national advertising; yet in cable th
national cable advertising ($760 million) represen
advertising. Compared to newspaper, radio, and
tration of local advertising markets is low (see fi

The situation depicted in the figure becomes
cable operators considering the trends toward loc
In 1986, network sales grew at 3% compared
growth. For cable, national sales increased 21%
crease in local advertising sales. Leading adverti
and Pepsi have voiced their growing preference

These trends suggest a changing role for the ca
has traditionally focused on quality of picture re
system manager now will have to act more like a
manager, with greater emphasis on advertiser su
advertising sales, the system manager will have
graphic quantification problems and must also
hurdle.

Figure 2.3
The Cable System

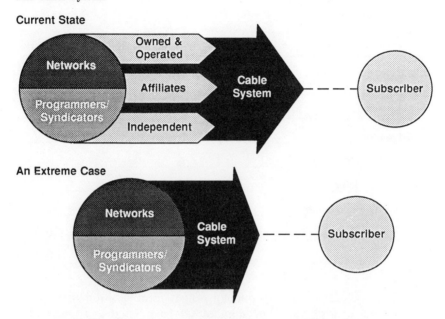

survey respondents were not clear about the profitability of interconnects, there was consensus support for linking cable systems via interconnects to attract advertising placements. Cable operators strongly favored "hard" interconnects to "soft" interconnects. (In "hard" interconnects, systems are directly linked by cable or microwave relays, and the signal is fed to the entire interconnect by one head-end (computer). In "soft' interconnects, there is no direct electronic connection between systems. Instead, commercials are inserted at approximately the same time by each participating system.) Hard (sometimes called "true") interconnects were considered more reliable and able to provide greater comfort to advertisers. All respondents felt that interconnects were a leading method to increase local advertising sales to major advertisers, the group most concerned with audience reach. One advertiser said, "Interconnects are like a godsend, because they enable you to go from dealing with ten cable operators to one entity."

MSO Programming

Unlike the networks, MSOs can participate in unlimited program development and distribution. Ownership of programming services enables the MSO to enjoy local *and* national advertising revenues along with local advertising revenues from external programming services.

Figure 2.4
Evaluation of Cable Systems

THE PROMISE
The table below summarizes where the promise is being fulfilled:

Promise	Excellent	Good	Fair
MSO Support	X		
Education	X		
Program Quality		X	
Basic Ad Sales		X	
Industry Positioning			X
Local Market Research			X
Local Ad Sales			X

MSO involvement in programming ranges from sponsorship through affiliate fees to program ownership. MSOs have acted as sponsors but increasingly are taking equity positions. Some say equity stakes in a programmer allow the MSO better control over the product it receives. For instance, Time Inc. (owner of ATC, HBO and Cinemax) recently took an equity position in Turner Broadcasting, the owner of WTBS and CNN. Many feel that Time's ultimate motive is control of CNN.

Summary: Where the Promise Is Being Fulfilled

Figure 2.4 summarizes where the promise is being fulfilled.

MSO Support—Excellent.

MSO support refers to dealings with basic programmers. MSOs have encouraged programmers to reinvest money in the services to increase the quality of programming and the viewer/advertiser attraction.

Education—Excellent.

Trade groups have made much progress in recent years to promote cable to agencies and advertisers. In particular, the Cable Advertising Bureau's Tune-In Kits have helped cable systems attract local advertising sales, and the Cable Planning System has supported agency analysis.

these regional networks is facing the problem that confronted pay programmers: justification of a premium charge.

The problems that pay networks are having in proving their price/value
relationship are well-documented. If the pay networks are having trouble
justifying an $8–$10 fee per month, most having 24-hour programming,
original production, and significant investment, it is hard to imagine sports
networks showing seven or less major live sports events a week attracting
that same type of value perception.

Regional broadcasters would be wise to focus more on advertiser support
and affiliate fees and less on direct subscriber charges. It would allow all
parties to benefit, as system operators strengthen the portfolio of basic
services, advertisers find an outlet for targeted geographic marketing with
larger reach, and consumers' price perception of cable service improves.

Market Research

Programmers, agencies, and advertisers face a number of market research hurdles. Quantitative data on cable viewership and demographics
are difficult to use, especially for agencies. Each of the 15 major basic
cable programming services provides the agencies with reports of varying
timeliness, daypart division and reporting by show. The inconsistencies
have caused confusion at the agencies, often creating a bias against younger
audiences. MTV has already conducted significant customized research,
including special Nielsen phone surveys.

Ratings interpretation is another problem. The confusion stems from
trying to integrate the different information resources that advertisers and
agencies must use to purchase time. To buy cable, they must combine the
1,700 household Nielsen Television Index meter samples, National Station
Index sweeps and National Audience Composition diary reports. It is a
logistical nightmare to find a quantitative justification for buying cable time.
The upcoming increased sample size of people-meter surveys is eagerly
awaited. It is in the cable programmers' best interest to hasten the process
of generating more simplified, quantified, and integrated market research.

Packaging

The basic programmer must decide whether to market to agencies or go
directly to advertisers. If programmers feel there is an agency bias against
cable, then marketing directly to the advertiser should be considered. Many
feel agencies view cable as a time-consuming, difficult buy and, therefore,
de-emphasize it in their media plans. Marketing to the advertiser may be
one way to combat this problem.

Cable time is sold by programmers by show and in packages of shows.
Bundling or unbundling sales will emerge as a critical topic. It is a debate

which some people are calling "run-of-system" versus "fixed-position" selling.

The consensus is that run-of-system—or bundled sales—is fine for a service like MTV, which has slightly less differentiated programming throughout the day. Programmers like MSG or ESPN, which clearly have certain shows with higher profiles and interest, cannot continue to bundle sales in the future. Frequently, MSG purchasers want to buy time on the New York teams, the Knicks and Rangers, but are forced to buy a mixed package of programming that often includes older syndicated shows. This is equivalent to asking an advertiser who wants to have a commercial placed during the Super Bowl to buy a bundled package of network times across dayparts, weeks and even months. If programmers like MSG and ESPN are going to become mature and independent advertising vehicles, they must prove the merit of each individual program.

Pricing

Basic programmers initially hoped to sell advertising time at premium rates per viewer. The more targeted, upscale cable audience was thought to be a prime deliverable to the agencies. This more affluent audience and its higher-than-average spending was seen as the answer to advertisers' prayers.

While reports from Mediamark Research Inc., the market research firm, confirm the higher-grade demographics on cable, advertising time continues to sell at a discounted rate or, in advertising jargon, "cost per thousand minus (CPM −)". Many of the people interviewed cited the lack of reliable, quantitative reporting about cable television as the prime hurdle confronting programmers, though help seems on the way. A. C. Nielsen's new Cable Audience Profile is the first recognized market research analysis to provide demographic information on a system-by-system basis. Those we interviewed questioned the report's timeliness and sampling technique, but generally applauded the effort and were optimistic about future refinements.

If cable programmers are going to become more than just secondary suppliers, they must improve on selling at CPM − and try to come nearer to parity with the stronger competitors. Programmers have to resist the temptation to market services at discounted rates in the short run if they are to break the "cheap channel" perception.

Local Advertising

Another recent study by Coopers and Lybrand, *Fine Tuning Cable Television*, identified local cable advertising as a leading source of revenue growth at the system level. In the opinion of 100 cable system managers,

Figure 2.2
1986 Advertising Revenues

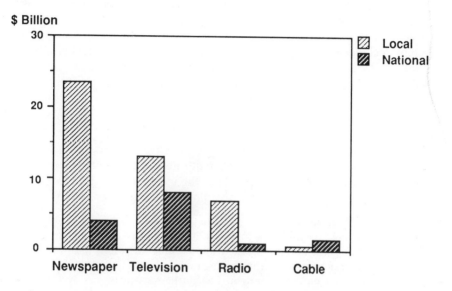

there are almost no more home runs to hit. They feel cable has become a singles and doubles game where advances come from incremental improvements to current activities. Cable advertising and pay-per-view programming were the only areas considered legitimate big-payoff candidates.

Local cable advertising is potentially the largest untapped revenue source for the MSO. For cable's competitors, local advertising is significantly more prevalent than national advertising; yet in cable the reverse is true. In 1986, national cable advertising ($760 million) represented about 80% of all cable advertising. Compared to newspaper, radio, and television, cable's penetration of local advertising markets is low (see figure 2.2).

The situation depicted in the figure becomes even more favorable for cable operators considering the trends toward local advertising placement. In 1986, network sales grew at 3% compared to local broadcast's 14% growth. For cable, national sales increased 21%, compared to a 35% increase in local advertising sales. Leading advertisers such as McDonald's and Pepsi have voiced their growing preference for local placements.

These trends suggest a changing role for the cable system manager, who has traditionally focused on quality of picture reception and billing. The system manager now will have to act more like a television station general manager, with greater emphasis on advertiser support. To encourage local advertising sales, the system manager will have to overcome the demographic quantification problems and must also overcome the education hurdle.

Most local advertisers are familiar with newspaper, local television, radio, and yellow page offerings, and are less acquainted with cable television. Very often cable is perceived as a source of movies and sports, but there is little recognition of specific stations and viewer groups. The cable system manager must increase awareness of cable attributes. An effective selling technique is marketing to specific product/service categories (e.g., banks, car dealers). Frequently, the presence of one company on cable will attract its competitors to the medium.

An Extreme Case

A few respondents felt that local cable advertising growth could take a quantum leap with the support of the major networks. They believed local cable systems could supplant the role of the local affiliate. Two incentives for the networks to consider new distribution partners were cited:

1. Affiliate compensation. In aggregate, the networks now pay approximately $500 million a year to affiliates to carry programming. This is in contrast to independent television stations, which have to pay for programming at ever increasing rates.
2. Programming preemption. Tension between networks and affiliates over preemption of network broadcast is at an all-time high. Affiliates have increasingly substituted original programming, for which they can insert their own advertising, for late-night and late-morning shows.

Respondents felt that if cable penetration could rise from its current level of approximately 50% to 65%, it would be viewed as a "mass market" distribution alternative. In some markets—most likely not the largest cities—the cable operators or a consortium of operators could be strong competition for local affiliates.

For instance, a Phoenix cable system could become the local distribution point in network programming, replacing the current practice of rebroadcasting affiliate feeds. A contract could be structured to meet the needs of the cable operator and the network. The cable operator most likely would get a number of valuable advertising slots, and the network could receive assurance of programming carriage and the elimination of compensation payments. Implementation of this type of arrangement would be technologically simple because most networks are now broadcasting via satellite.

Figure 2.3 depicts the current distribution system and the "extreme case" just discussed.

Interconnects

Whether cable becomes a network program distributor or not, interconnects are crucial to the success of local advertising sales efforts. While

Program Quality—Good.

The promise of more innovative and diverse programming is being fulfilled. Frequently, programming originates on cable and migrates to the network. Examples are the big splash made by the "Max Headroom" show aired on ABC and the success of the comedian Gary Shandling, who started on cable and now guest hosts "The Tonight Show". ESPN's purchase of NFL games has also enhanced cable's image.

Basic Advertising Sales—Good.

The growth rate of national cable advertising sales is quite significant considering the flattened growth in network sales. Survey respondents express some concern about whether high growth rates will persist.

Industry Positioning—Fair.

The debate on mass appeal versus targeted marketing continues. Industry image consensus will help spur future growth.

Local Market Research—Fair.

Local market research seems to be the major hurdle for reaching the untapped market. Progress has been made but has yet to have a significant effect.

Local Ad Sales—Fair.

In part, this is a cultural issue, as many systems simply are not marketing local availability. The maturation of cable systems should lead to increased emphasis on this revenue stream.

The advertising hope for cable was still strong in our survey; programmers and MSOs must fulfill that hope. They must continue to increase the awareness of cable attributes, provide better quantitative support of claims, unify the selling image and deliver higher quality programming.

In summary, cable advertising has experienced great growth, but it has yet to fulfill its promise completely. Greater attention to positioning, research, and local advertising issues is necessary in order for that to happen.

3

Programming Holes: Opportunities for Cable Networks

Roland T. Rust and Naveen Donthu

Introduction

For many years the television environment in the United States was ruled by the three major networks: ABC, CBS, and NBC. In some large cities independent stations enjoyed a sizable share of the audience, but generally speaking the networks' combined share of audience was very large. As recently as 1977 the estimated network share of the prime time audience was 91%.

Cable television began as a way of providing programming to isolated, rural communities. In the last ten years, however, cable penetration has exploded from only 19% of U.S. households in 1979, through over 41% of U.S. households in 1985 (Television Digest, 1985), to an estimated 50% by 1988. Projections of 1990 cable penetration range from 54% (DMB&B, 1986) to 58% (Kaatz, 1985), and a conservative projection estimates a 64% penetration by the year 2000 (Krugman and Rust, 1987).

A result of the growth in cable penetration has been a decrease in the audience share enjoyed by the three networks. From 91% in 1977 it had steadily fallen to 72% in 1985, and is projected to decline to 61% in 1990 and 54% in 2000 (Krugman and Rust, 1987).

It is clear that cable is becoming an increasingly important player in the television game. Cable's growing audience will bring in higher advertising revenue, all other things being equal. In fact, the increase in cable revenue should outstrip its increase in audience, due to a rising trend in the revenue generated per cable household, even after adjusting for inflation (Krugman and Rust, 1987).

These financial trends indicate that the cable environment is likely to be very dynamic in the coming years, with many new channels formed, many old channels dying, and many existing channels renovated to cope with competitive pressures. An important question is: how should a cable channel plan its programming in order to compete successfully?

Marketers talk about this issue as being "product positioning." What is referred to is the position of a product in perceptual space. In other words, two products that are very similar will be close to each other in perceptual space, while two very different products will be far apart.

All other things being equal, it is advantageous to be positioned uniquely, with no close competitors, since that means the product will monopolize that part of the market. Cable theorists have realized this for a long time. They have spoken of cable programming as "narrowcasting," aiming for a small audience segment, rather than "broadcasting" to the masses. From a financial standpoint this makes a great deal of sense. The cable channels lack the financial resources to compete head-to-head with the major networks for the mass audience. Therefore they instead seek smaller, more specialized audiences whose needs they can meet more completely.

The problem for the cable channel then is how to locate an appropriate market niche. What programming needs are not currently being satisfied by the existing cable lineup? To answer this question we must first map the audience's perceptual space, find out where the existing channels are perceived to be, and then position the cable channel where it will have the most viewers and the least competition.

The Strategic Approach

Imagine three television viewers: Doug, Judy, and Mark. Doug is a sports fan. He watches major sports events on the major networks, and also enjoys watching ESPN regularly. Judy, on the other hand, prefers the fine arts, and spends most of her viewing hours watching PBS and the Arts Network. Mark is a movie buff. He watches network movie presentations, and often tunes to HBO and Cinemax.

Let us assume that most people perceive programs in the same way (although they may not prefer the same programs). In perceptual space, then, most sports programs would be grouped close together, movie programs would be grouped together, and arts programs would tend to be grouped together. It is useful to imagine viewers mapped in the same space. For example Doug would be mapped close to the sports programs he watches, Judy close to the arts programs, and Mark close to the movies.

If a cable channel is to have a unique identity, in order to narrowcast successfully, it must also occupy a specific position in perceptual space. For example, ESPN undoubtedly intends to be perceived as similar to network sports broadcasts. It would then be positioned in perceptual space close to the network sports programs, and would probably be attractive to viewers like Doug.

In other words, we may imagine a space which contains viewers, network programs, and cable channels, with viewers tending to watch network programs and cable channels which are close to their "ideal points." A new or repositioned cable channel would then seek to position itself in perceptual space close to as many viewer ideal points as possible, yet as far from competing cable channels as possible.

The density of the viewer ideal points may be visualized as a surface with mountains and valleys. Mountains would be places in the perceptual space where there are many viewers, and valleys would be where there are few viewers. It would be best for a cable channel to position itself in a "mountainous area" unless there is too much competition there.

Finding the best positioning involves trading off potential audience against existing competitive strength. The next section outlines a mathematical method for doing this in order to obtain an optimal market position.

But how does the optimal market position translate to programming? The prescribed market position may be characterized by the programs and networks which are close to it. For example, if ESPN and network sports programs were near the optimal market position, the indication would be that a new sports channel was in order. On the other hand, if the new position were between network movies and fine arts programs, then the indication might be to have an art and foreign film network.

Repositioning is also interpretable in this way. For example, suppose ESPN's suggested optimal repositioning would move it in the direction of network golf broadcasts. That would be a signal to show more golf.

The next section discusses some of the techniques that may be used to implement this strategic approach.

Methodology

In order to capture consumers' perception of competing cable channels, we propose to use multidimensional scaling. Multidimensional scaling is a set of procedures designed to spatially represent proximities between a number of stimuli. It transforms unidimensional expressions of relationships into multidimensional expressions of the same relationships. The appendix to this chapter describes how multidimensional scaling works, for those readers not already familiar with that technique.

Any phenomenon (product, service, image, aroma, etc.) can be thought of as having both perceived dimensions and objective dimensions. Multidimensional scaling techniques enable researchers/managers to represent these dimensions spatially; to create visual displays that represent the dimensions perceived by the respondents while evaluating stimuli (brands, objects, etc.). This visual depiction helps the researcher to better understand similarities and dissimilarities between objective and perceptual dimensions.

When individual perceptions of stimuli are obtained from respondents, a wide variety of techniques or procedures may be used, but the resulting data may be generally categorized as preference data, similarity data (proximity data), or ideal points. These data serve as the basis for using multidimensional scaling techniques to derive the perceptual dimensions used by the respondents to judge the similarity of and preference for ideal stimuli.

An ideal point represents the most preferred combination of perceived attributes (on all relevant attribute dimensions). The position of the ideal point on this perceptual map would also be related to relative preference of all other stimuli. The ideal point position is determined by the assumption that the rank order of preference for a subject should correspond to the rank order of the distances of the stimuli from the position of the subject's ideal point.

Ideal point models, which jointly map the products under consideration and the consumer ideal points, are widely used in marketing to develop product positioning and segmentation strategies. These joint maps help to identify gaps or opportunities in the market and to determine whether these positions will generate adequate demand. This technique helps capture individual differences in preference, which is of prime importance to cable programmers.

Some of the scaling algorithms developed in recent years include ALSCAL (Takane, Young, and de Leeuw, 1977), MULTISCAL (Ramsey, 1977), the "Probabilistic" approach (Zinnes and MacKay, 1983), and the "Pick-Any" algorithm (Levine, 1979).

Proposals for heuristic solutions of the positioning problem based on the joint map of products and ideal points have been made by Kuehn and Day (1962), Pessemier (1975), Shocker and Srinivasan (1974), Urban (1975), Brockhoff and Albers (1977), and Zufryden (1979), to name a few. These approaches, which give an analytical formulation of the problem, differ mainly in the underlying behavioral hypotheses.

Shocker and Srinivasan assume that the distance between the ideal points and the perceived location of the product is associated with a purchase probability less than one and greater than zero. On the other hand Brockhoff and Albers, and Zufryden, base their models on the assumption that a consumer chooses the product which is closest to his/her ideal point with a probability of one. DeSarbo and Hoffman (1986) propose a threshold unfolding model where a product is chosen whenever it is closer than a critical (threshold) distance.

Gavish, Horsky, and Srikanth (1983) consider a joint space of ideal points and products, and plot consumer indifference curves, which are elliptical in shape. The shape of the ellipses are determined by the importance a consumer places on the attributes. They show that the optimal location for positioning a product is at the intersection of the maximum number of ellipses. Hence if the product is placed within the indifference ellipse for a consumer, it is assumed that he/she will choose it.

From the point of view of a continuous density function of ideal points, the models described above all estimate market share for product locations as though they assume that there is positive density only at the sample ideal points. It is intuitively reasonable to expect a positive density of ideal points all over the space, and especially in the areas near the existing sample ideal points. The density model used in this paper has been used to position radio stations (Donthu, Rust, and Lynch, 1987) and to evaluate market areas (Donthu and Rust, 1987).

From the density function point of view, most current positioning models assume density "spikes," representing positive density only at the ideal points, with a zero density elsewhere. By contrast, the nonparametric density approach smooths these spikes by assigning some probability of having ideal points to the region around the sample ideal points. Figure 3.1 illustrates the density estimation depiction of the direct ideal point approach, and figure 3.2 shows the corresponding density of the ideal points calculated by nonparametric density estimation (to be discussed elsewhere in this section).

It is usually very difficult to make a priori assumptions about the distribution of these ideal points. In the past Benson (1965) used hypothetical distributions of consumer ideal points, while Kamakura and Srivastava (1986) assumed that the ideal points within a segment were normally distributed. In this paper we use a very flexible method of density estimation known as kernel density estimation. This method of density estimation can flexibly capture various shapes based on the distribution of the ideal points in the joint map of products and ideal points.

The Proposed Method

The proposed model uses a joint map of consumer ideal points and perceived locations of competing cable channels as an input. We assume that this is given by a multidimensional unfolding algorithm using viewing preference data. The model then estimates the density function of the ideal points and uses that to estimate audience shares for various possible channel positionings. The model may be used to estimate the optimal location for a new or repositioned product.

We will first discuss the kernel density estimation technique and then discuss the mathematics of the proposed density model for flexible ideal point density estimation and product positioning.

Figure 3.1
Direct Ideal Point Approach: The Density Function of the Ideal Points as Spikes at the Sample Ideal Points

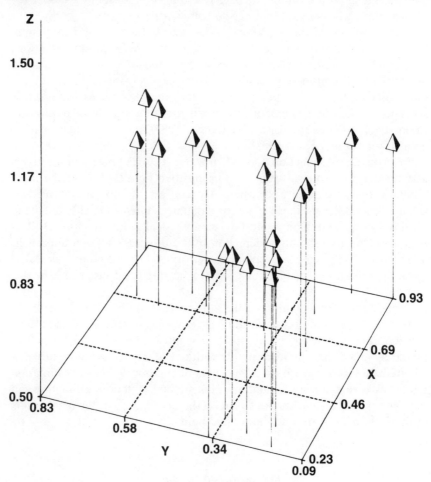

Kernel Density Estimation

Most of the literature on density estimation is of a highly technical nature with little consideration for possible application. Useful sources which give the flavor of the subject from various points of view are Boneva, Kendall and Stefanov (1971), Wegman (1972), Rosenblatt (1971), Fryer (1977), and Silverman (1986).

The contemporary study of fully non-parametric density estimates began

Figure 3.2
Nonparametric Density Estimation Approach: The Density Function of the Ideal
Points as a Smooth Function of the Sample Ideal Points

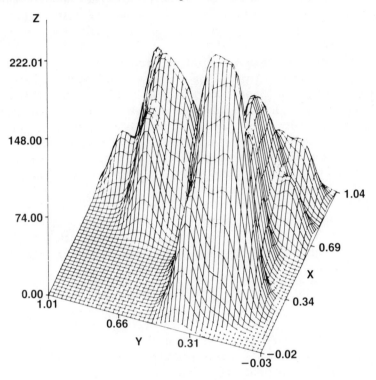

with Rosenblatt (1971), who first explicitly introduced the kernel estimate.
The kernel density, f(x), is defined in d dimensions as:

$$f(x) = (nh^d)^{-1}\sum_{i=1}^{n} K(x-x_i)/h,$$

where K is the kernel function, h is the smoothing factor or window width,
n is the number of data points, and x_i are the data points.

If the kernel function is defined for all values of x, then f(x) has a positive
density over the entire space. The density is the sum of n kernel functions,
each centered at the observed points. Regions of the space in which there
are many data points have a high density, while regions in which there are
few points have a low density. The actual estimation, however, is continuous and not by regions.

The choice of the kernel function and smoothing factor are to some extent arbitrary. The choice of an optimal kernel function was considered by Epanechnikov (1969) and Silverman (1986). They showed that the choice of the kernel function is not very crucial and most functions, including normal and uniform, give near optimal results, even with small sample sizes.

The smoothing parameter h dictates to what extent the density surface will follow the data. A large h results in a smooth-looking surface, while a small h results in a more lumpy surface. The problem of objectively choosing the value of h is a subject of current research, and several objective and partially objective methods have been suggested; see for example, Woodroofe (1970), Parzen (1979), and Silverman (1986).

Density estimation techniques have been used for many years in statistics and mathematics for exploratory analysis, confirmatory analysis, and data presentation. Application in marketing and marketing research have included market area analysis (Rust and Brown, 1986; Donthu and Rust, 1987), nonparametric regression (Rust, 1987), and conjoint analysis (Brown and Donthu, 1987). The technique suggests itself naturally for flexibly estimating the density of ideal points to develop an aggregate model of choice.

Audience Share Estimation

Given the estimated density function of the ideal points, along with assumptions about how distance is related to choice, we may then estimate market share for any product location in the joint space.

The probability $P_{ij'}$, that person i selects channel j', is assumed to be the ratio of utility of channel j' to the total utility of all J channels under consideration (Luce, 1959; Schonmann and Wang, 1972):

$$P_{ij} = \frac{U_{ij'}}{\sum_{j-1}^{J} U_{ij}} \tag{1}$$

This formulation has been previously used in several models (e.g., Schonmann and Wang, 1972; Shocker and Srinivasan, 1974).

The joint Euclidean distance between subject i and cable channel j obtained from the unfolding map (Coombs, 1964) is:

$$d_{ij} = \sum_{k=1}^{K} (x_{ik} - y_{jk})^2 \tag{2}$$

Hence the distance between the ideal points and the channels can be determined using (2), where X_{ik} and y_{jk} are locations of subject i' and channel j respectively. Finally, we postulate that these distances d_{ij} relate to utility U_{ij} as:

$$U_{ij} = \exp(-c\, d_{ij}^2) \tag{3}$$

where c is a constant between 0 and 1. This formulation has been used by Schonmann and Wang (1972). A different relationship might just as easily be used and should not invalidate the proposed method.

Now for cable channel j' under consideration, the audience share is estimated by integrating the product of the density and the probability across the entire surface:

$$\text{Audience Share } ASj' = \int_{R}^{k} g(x)\, P_{ij'}\, dx \tag{4}$$

where $g(x)$ is not known, but may be estimated using nonparametric density estimation.

Substituting P_{ij} (from (2)) in (4) yields:

$$ASj' = \int_{R}^{k} g(x)\, \frac{\exp[-c((x_{i1} - mj) + (x_{i2} - nj')^2)]}{\sum_{j} \exp[-c((x_{i1} - mj) + (x_{i2} - nj)^2)]}\, dx \tag{5}$$

The expression for market share in (5) may be estimated using a fine grid (as it does not have a closed form solution). Hence given the density function $g(x)$ of the ideal points, and the perceived locations (mj, nj) of the existing channels in the same map, it is possible to estimate the audience share for a new cable channel location (mj', nj') in the same place.

Differentiating the expression (5) with respect to mj and nj respectively and setting them equal to zero we can approximate the optimal location for a new or repositioned cable station. The resulting location will maximize the market share for this new station. This process involves Taylor series approximation of the market share and Newton-Raphson method of numerical optimization (Donthu, 1986).

An Illustrative Example

To demonstrate the potential usefulness of the methodology described in the previous data, we obtained data from a sample of 150 households from a medium-sized southwestern city. The example is for illustrative purposes only, and no claims are made regarding its generalizability to the national cable audience. National application would require several refinements, such as obtaining a national sample and making provisions for the unavailability of particular cable channels in some markets. Nevertheless the analysis presented here should be suggestive of what a larger-scale analysis might accomplish.

We collected viewing preference data from a systematic random sample

Figure 3.3
Joint Map of Ideal Points (150) and Cable Television Channels (14)

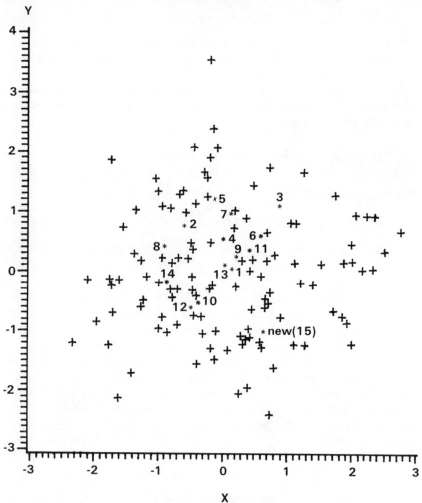

of respondents in a large southwestern city. The data were collected using telephone interviews. Respondents were included in the study only if they received cable service.

The respondents were first asked to list four of their favorite network and public television programs. Second, they were provided with a list of fourteen cable television channels and were asked to evaluate each of these on a scale of one to five. A score of five represented that they were very likely to view that cable channel, and a score of one represented that they were not very likely to view that cable channel. They were also required to identify channels they did not receive or with which they were not

Table 3.1
Market Share Estimation for Cable Television Channels

Channel Number	Channel Name	Estimated Market Share	Estimated Market Share After #15 Enters the Market
1	LIFETIME	7.65	5.62
2	ESPN	5.20	5.15
3	CNN	6.06	5.45
4	USA	3.57	3.28
5	WTBS	4.23	4.38
6	NICK	4.64	3.62
7	INDEPENDENT	2.58	2.51
8	MTV	7.09	6.94
9	DISNEY	5.59	3.87
10	CINEMAX	13.58	10.52
11	A&E	5.63	3.70
12	HBO	14.82	12.04
13	GALAVISION	7.91	6.00
14	SHOWTIME	11.26	10.64
15	NEW CHANNEL	--.--	16.26

familiar. Demographic data such as sex, age, student/non-student, and home zip code were also collected for classification purposes.

The ratings data regarding the cable stations were used as an input to the ALSCAL (Takane, Young, and de Leeuw, 1977) unfolding algorithm, which provided the joint map of respondent ideal points and the 14 cable channels used in this study. The joint map is presented in figure 3.3. The numbers (one through fourteen) represent the cable channels listed in table 3.1. Other details on this table will be discussed later in this section.

From the density function perspective, the ideal point model would represent each of these sample ideal points as a spike to estimate the market share for the various locations in space. However, the density model proposed in this paper uses the estimated density function of these ideal points. The kernel density function of the ideal points is shown in figure 3.4. Figure

Figure 3.4
Kernel Density Map of Ideal Points

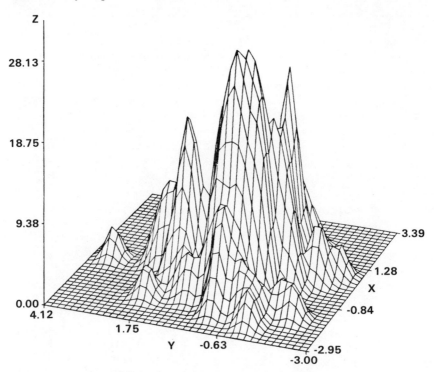

3.5 is the corresponding contour map of the kernel density map. This gives us an alternative picture of the density of the ideal points.

The density model was used to estimate the market shares for all cable channels used in this study. Table 3.1 shows the audience share predictions using the density approach. It is important to note that these estimates are based on the small sample used in the study and assume that the market consists of these 14 cable stations only. Hence the estimated figures may not match the published shares.

Now assuming that a new cable channel has decided to enter the market, we deal with the issue of positioning this new channel to maximize the share of the cable audience. We will also identify network programs that are associated with this new channel location, in order to make the positioning strategy meaningful.

The estimated optimal location for the new channel 15 is shown in figure 3.3. The predicted change in the market's market share structure after station 15 enters the market is shown in table 3.1. This position is predicted to draw customers away from existing cable channels and provide the new channel with maximum audience share.

Figure 3.5
Contour Map of Density of Ideal Points

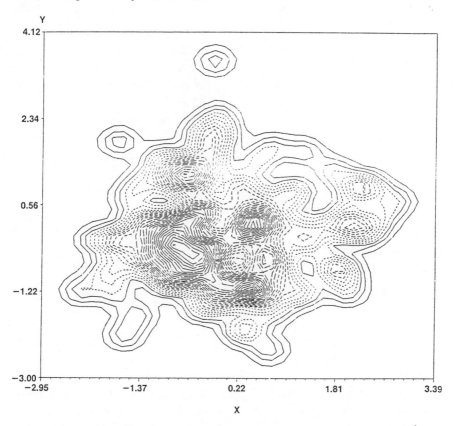

It would also be possible to maximize other criteria, such as advertising revenue, instead of audience share. That would involve weighting the respondents appropriately. For example, if high ratings in the women 18–49 age group were advantageous in increasing ad revenues, then respondents in that segment could be weighted as greater. The remainder of the approach would remain exactly the same.

It is not always necessary that a cable channel reposition itself to maximize its market share. For any location (including suboptimal ones) the model may be used to predict the audience share. Figures 3.6 and 3.7 are the plots of expected market share for the new cable channel at different locations in the space. From the figures it is clear that the optimum location determined by the proposed algorithm is indeed the global optimum.

It is also important that the manager of the cable channel understand what the optimal location means. In this application, network and public television programs are used to describe locations in the space. Hence

Figure 3.6
Expected Market Share for New Cable Television Channel

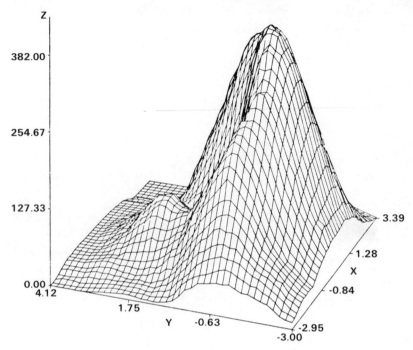

unlike other MDS applications it is not very important to name directions (or dimensions) in the space. Here it is more important to associate cable channel locations in space with images of television programs.

The favorite television programs listed by the respondents were placed at the centroids of the respondents who listed them. For each cable channel the list of programs associated with its prescribed location in the perceptual space was determined using the plot of the distance of the program from the channel versus the conditional probability that a channel will be chosen given that the program is chosen. The conditional probability is the ratio of the number who listed the program and were very likely to watch the cable channel to the total number of people who listed the program. An exponentially decreasing curve was fitted to the data (see figure 3.8).

Figure 3.8 is an illustration of the probability versus distance plot discussed above. Here on the horizontal axis we have distances of the program from the channel in the map; and on the vertical axis we have the probability associated with each program. All programs to the left of the dotted line are closely associated with the location of the cable channel under consideration; hence they are associated with the channel.

Given the fitted exponential curve, a program was inferred to be asso-

Figure 3.7
Contour Map of Expected Market Share for New Cable Television Channel

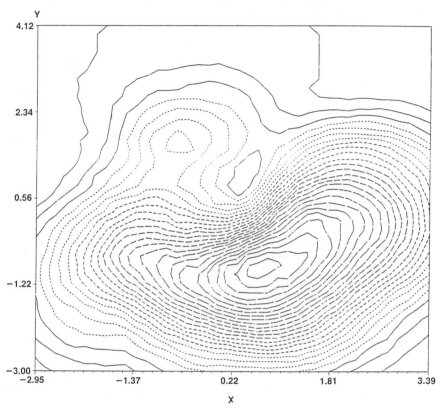

ciated with a channel if the inferred conditional probability exceeded 0.5. Geometrically this means that we may construct a circle around each channel location, with programs found within the circle inferred as associated with the channel. This provides a surrogate for channel identity. As a result, each cable channel's image may be characterized by its set of associated network or public television programs.

In the case of the new cable channel the following television programs were strongly associated with its location on the perceptual map: (1) "60 Minutes," (2) "Nightline," (3) "Magnum P.I.," (4) "Mike Hammer," (5) "Murder She Wrote." Hence this location was perceived to be associated with investigative news reporting programs or action/mystery shows.

This could be used to design the programming content of the new cable station. The programming implication would be that either a news channel or an action/mystery entertainment channel should be contemplated.

Figure 3.8
Illustration of Methodology to Determine Television Programs Associated with a Station's Location in the Perceptual Map

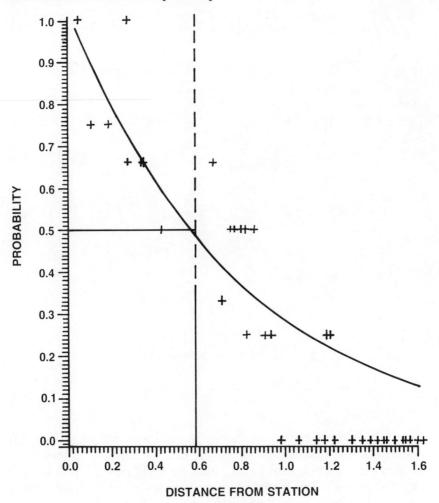

Summary and Conclusions

This chapter describes how a new or existing cable channel may identify a programming hole and use that information to position (or reposition) the channel's programming. The general idea is to supply programming for viewers whose needs are not currently being met. It is assumed that a cable channel, unlike the major broadcast networks, should seek to occupy a very narrow, specific market niche.

It is shown how survey data may be used to produce a map which simultaneously maps viewers, network programs, and cable channels. From this map, the distribution of viewing preferences in the population is estimated. Based on the estimated preference distribution, a cable channel may consider the projected ratings implications of revised programming. A new or existing cable channel may also investigate the programming image that will produce the greatest audience share or share of revenues.

Because of the rapid increase in cable television's share of the viewing audience and cable's increasing share of television revenue, cable television programming is a dynamic decision area which is growing in importance. This chapter overviews an approach for using research to help make timely programming decisions in the rapidly evolving cable television environment.

Appendix:
Review of Multidimensional Scaling

Naveen Donthu and Roland T. Rust

Introduction

Multidimensional scaling is a family of statistical procedures for transforming unidimensional expressions of relationships into multidimensional expressions. In essence, multidimensional scaling (hereafter referred to as MDS) is a data reduction technique that is primarily concerned with uncovering the hidden structure of a set of data. A distinguishing feature of MDS is that it provides a visual representation of a reduced set of data which is often easier to interpret than the data itself (Hair et al., 1979).

As a mathematical tool, MDS allows a researcher to represent the proximities (similarities) between objects on a perceptual map. The input for MDS is typically either proximities data, which indicate similarities or differences between pairs of objects, or preference data, which represent certain rankings of objects.

The primary objective of MDS is to map objects in a multidimensional space such that the relative positions of the objects reflect the degree of proximity (i.e., similarity) between all possible pairs of objects. To illustrate how MDS reaches this objective, an example is provided.

Consider a marketing research problem where an analyst wants to determine how consumers perceive a set of soft drinks. One method of researching this problem is to ask consumers overt questions such as, "Which soft drinks are the sweetest?" or "Which soft drinks taste the best?" The problem with this approach is that the attributes upon which the stimuli (soft drinks) are being evaluated have been defined by the researcher. These attributes may or may not reflect the true criteria used by consumers to evaluate the product.

MDS allows a researcher to determine consumer perceptions without the use of predefined product attributes. This is achieved by having the subjects in a study evaluate the soft drinks in terms of similarity or preference. For example, a researcher could present subjects with a set of cards, each of which contains the names of two soft drinks. Subjects would be asked to rank order the cards with respect to similarity such that the first card represents the most similar pair, the second card represents the

Figure 3.9
Illustrative Two-Dimensional MDS Output

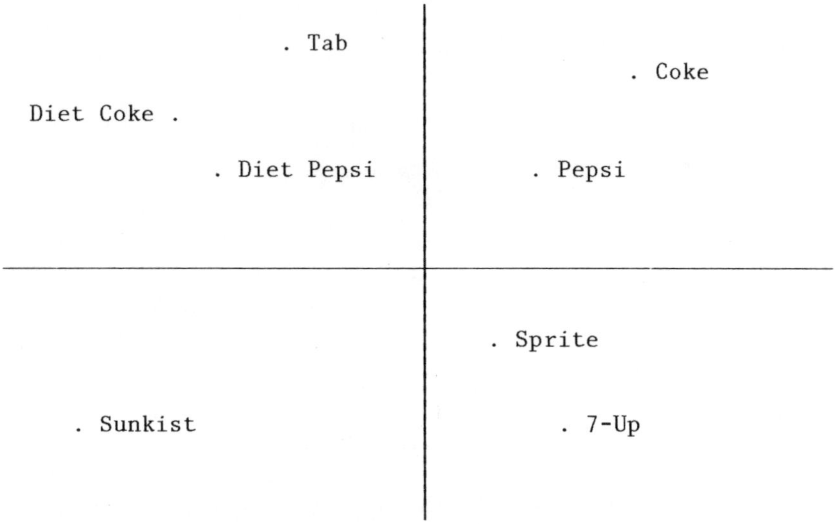

```
                    . Tab         |
                                  |                . Coke
        Diet Coke .               |
                                  |
            . Diet Pepsi          |        . Pepsi
                                  |
                                  |
    _____|_____
                                  |
                                  |        . Sprite
                                  |
        . Sunkist                 |           . 7-Up
                                  |
                                  |
                                  |
```

next most similar pair, and so on until the last card, which represents the least similar pair. The similarity judgments are then constructed into a matrix representing the rank orders of the similarities of each pair of soft drinks. This matrix is then input into an MDS computer program.

The MDS algorithm produces an output which includes a visual representation of the original data in some of a certain number of dimensions, say R dimensions. A two-dimensional output of the soft drink case is shown in figure 3.9.

The researcher must then interpret the map in an attempt to explain the relative positions of the points. In the above configuration, the horizontal axis could be labeled diet/nondiet because objects appear to be spread out horizontally according to this attribute. The vertical axis could be labeled cola/noncola in a similar fashion. Observe that products appearing the upper right quadrant, Coke and Pepsi, are nondiet cola drinks. Products in the upper left quadrant, Tab, Diet Coke, and Diet Pepsi, are diet cola drinks.

An MDS output allows a researcher to determine what soft drinks are similar to what other soft drinks and what attributes consumers use to evaluate soft drinks. This simple illustration provides a brief sketch of what MDS does. In actual use, MDS is far more sophisticated.

Development of MDS

MDS was first proposed by Young and Householder (1938) and Richardson (1938). However, the seminal works in application of MDS were done by

Figure 3.10
MDS Input Modes

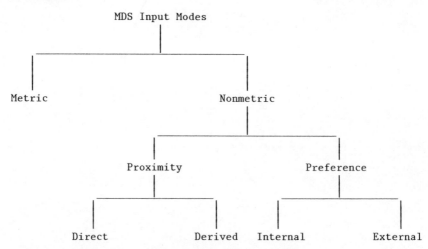

Shepard (1962) and Kruskal (1964). Shepard developed a computer algorithm for MDS that accepted ordinal input data. Kruskal expanded Shepard's work and developed a method of measuring how well a configuration represents a set of proximities data.

Applications in marketing were introduced by Green (1970), Green and Carmone (1969, 1972) and Neidell (1969) among others. More recent developments have focused on the use of MDS for specific applications such as product positioning (Donthu and Rust, 1988), market segmentation (Wind, 1978) and the simultaneous mapping of various entities (Keon, 1983).

There are many different types of MDS procedures, which vary with respect to whether the input data are metric or nonmetric and whether they are proximal or preference. The breakdown of MDS input modes is depicted in figure 3.10.

Fully metric methods require ratio-scaled distances as input. MDS uses ratio-scaled distances to find a configuration whose interpoint distances are proportional to the input data. Fully metric methods are based on a set of theorems proved by Young and Householder (1938). Torgenson (1958) developed the first completely workable method for metric MDS. This method, also known as classical scaling, is quite similar to principal components analysis in that the distance measures are converted to scalar products. Fully metric methods are seldom used today because of their restrictive assumptions and the difficulty of collecting metric input data.

MDS procedures that are fully nonmetric do not assume more than rank order of input distances. The objective of these methods is to find a space of minimum dimensionality and determine the rank order of each point on each dimension in turn (Green and Carmone, 1970). Fully nonmetric methods do not provide a configuration of points in space. Rather, they provide a rank order of stimulus projections on each dimension. These methods were developed by Coombs (1952) and Bennett and Hays (1960).

The drawback of fully nonmetric techniques is that they provide nonmetric output, which does not contain much information. In practice, these methods are not very operational; but they are important since they provide a conceptual basis for other methods.

Nonmetric methods combine the best of the above two approaches. Nonmetric methods accept rank ordered (ordinal) input data and find a configuration whose rank order of ratio-scaled distances best produces the original input ranks. The breakthrough achieved by nonmetric MDS is the conversion of nonmetric input into ratio-scaled output. Nonmetric programs apply monotone transformations to the original data through a sophisticated algorithm so as to permit arithmetic operations to be performed on the data. Shepard (1962) demonstrated that it was possible to derive metric MDS solutions assuming only an ordinal relationship between proximities and distances. Shepard also provided the first computer program for MDS, which was nonmetric. Kruskal (1964) built on Shepard's work by establishing a systematic method for optimizing the goodness-of-fit between the original data and the output configuration.

Given a particular set of data that meets the input requirements of both metric and nonmetric MDS, the solution of each method is quite similar. It is not uncommon for a researcher working with metric input data to run two MDS programs, one metric and one nonmetric.

Data Collection Techniques

Nonmetric MDS can be subdivided based on the type of data that are input into MDS. Input data can either be proximity (consonance) data or preference (dominance) data. While MDS performs the same general procedures on both types of data, there are considerable differences in the methods by which type of data are collected and prepared for analysis.

A proximity is a number which indicates how similar or different two objects are, or are perceived to be. Typical proximity data input is a rank ordering of pairs of stimuli on the basis of similarity. For example, a subject may be asked to develop a rank ordered list of stimulus pairs of ten soft drinks. The first pair would represent the most similar pair of soft drinks while the last pair would represent the least similar pair. MDS produces a configuration that reflects the relationship among the stimulus objects in some multidimensional space.

This type of data is prepared for input by creating a symmetrical, square matrix in which both the rows and the columns represent stimulus objects.

Each cell in the matrix indicates the rank order in terms of similarity for a particular pair of stimuli.

When a single proximity data matrix is input into MDS, it is known as "two-way" MDS since the input matrix has two dimensions. However, it is common for proximities to be collected from many subjects. As a result, a series of matrices are input into the algorithm. When this occurs, the term "three-way" MDS is used since the input matrix has three dimensions—two for the stimuli and one for the subjects.

Proximities data can be collected in a variety of ways, which can be classified as either direct or derived. Direct similarity collection techniques occur when subjects are asked to evaluate pairs of objects in terms of similarity. Derived data collection techniques involve the derivation of similarities from some other measure.

In direct similarity collection methods, subjects are presented with stimulus pairs and asked to judge their similarity. A major advantage of this method is that the use of verbal descriptors is avoided. Verbal descriptors such as adjectives are highly subjective and often conceptually incomplete. Since MDS attempts to uncover the hidden structure of the data, direct similarity collection techniques are especially appropriate in that subjects are not biased by the existence of certain criteria or descriptors.

Proximity data can be collected in a second manner in which a researcher derives similarity of stimuli from some other measure. For example, a researcher could have subjects rate each of a set of stimuli on a set of semantic differential scales.

The input data are then arranged in a rectangular matrix with columns representing stimuli (e.g., soft drinks) and rows representing subjects (people). Similarities between stimuli can then be calculated by comparing the rows of the matrix and determining the association between the rankings of different subjects. The most common ways to derive profile proximity measures are to compute correlations between variables or squared distances between stimuli.

The second major area for applications of MDS is preference data. In preference data, stimuli are ordered with respect to some property where relationships connoting "greater than" or "less than" can be depicted. Preference data imply the existence of a continuum on which stimuli can be evaluated (Bechtel, 1976).

The objective of preference MDS is to represent both subjects and stimuli on the same visual configuration such that inferences can be drawn about the subjects or stimuli, or both (Green and Carmone, 1970). Subjects are represented in space by what are known as ideal points, which indicate the combination of attributes (dimensions) optimally preferred by the subject. The closer a stimulus is to a subject's ideal point, the more it is preferred. Conversely, the further a stimulus is from an ideal point, the less it is preferred.

Coombs (1964) was the first to develop the concept of ideal points. Coombs also developed a procedure for "unfolding" a set of preference data to produce the rank order of the stimuli. The expression, "unfolding analysis" refers to a situation where preference data are unfolded to obtain a joint space of persons and stimuli such that the rank order of the stimulus distances from each ideal point corresponds to the original preference data (Green and Carmone, 1969).

MDS models for preference data were classified as either internal or external by Carroll (1972). In internal analysis, both stimulus and subject parameters are unknown and must be estimated. In external analysis, the stimulus coordinates are known and only subject parameters must be estimated.

There are a variety of approaches to collecting preference data that can be utilized in MDS. These techniques include many of the ordering techniques that can be used for proximities data as well as stimuli rating methods and rating methods that combine stimuli and subjects' ideal points.

How MDS Works

MDS achieves a configuration of points through an interactive process in which points are spatially moved in each iteration in an attempt to achieve a satisfactory representation of the proximities data. After each iteration, MDS computes a goodness-of-fit measure to see how closely the map fits the input data. The final, or terminal, iteration is reached when the improvement in stress does not exceed a predetermined level. The most commonly used goodness-of-fit measure is stress. Stress will be discussed in greater detail later.

Since MDS is a data reduction technique, its value lies in its ability to represent a set of data in a reduced dimensionality. That is, one that can be interpreted by the researcher. It can be shown that n points can always be represented in n–1 dimensions. This is true because any two points can be connected by a line and thus are represented in a single dimension.

Given that a set of n stimuli can be perfectly represented in a configuration of n–1 dimensions, MDS attempts to represent a set of n points in fewer than n–1 dimensions by sacrificing some of the exactness of the configuration's goodness-of-fit. Reducing the number of dimensions is possible because nonmetric MDS maintains only the rank order of the input data. For example, if the pair of points AB is more similar than the pair AC, then the distance between mapped points A and B should be less than the distance between points A and C.

It is important to note that MDS does not account for the degree of difference between the pairs of points. MDS is only concerned with maintaining the ordinal relationships among the original proximities. MDS actually converts ordinal input data into metric output data by spatially representing rank order data such that the distance between stimuli in the output configuration can be measured on a ratio scale.

The output of MDS is a visual configuration in some reduced dimensionality that preserves the ordered relationships of the stimuli as closely as possible. Frequently, MDS produces a two- or three-dimensional map since lower dimensionality facilitates interpretation. The researcher then attempts to explain the positioning of the points on some criterion.

As discussed previously, MDS proceeds through a series of iterations until an acceptable goodness-of-fit is achieved. A common index of the goodness-of-fit between the derived distances and the original proximities is Kruskal's "stress" value which represents the square root of a normalized residual sum of squares.

In practice, MDS starts out with an initial configuration, which may be determined randomly, then alters the configuration to minimize the stress measure, subject to the constraint of maintaining the monotonic relationships of the disparities. The terminal iteration is reached when the stress value fails to improve by a specified amount from the previous measure.

Stress is a crucial element of MDS because it is closely related to the dimensionality of the output configuration and is frequently the criterion upon which the final configuration is selected. Note that stress ranges from zero to one with goodness-of-fit being inversely related to the size of the stress. That is, low stress values indicate good fit. While there is no universal cutoff for determining what is an appropriate stress level, it is generally perceived that a stress value below 0.10 is acceptable.

Interpretation of the MDS Configuration

It has already been shown that MDS produces a perceptual map as output. This output does not provide explicit information about a set of proximities or preferences. Rather, it is up to the researcher to interpret the relative positions of points by determining the dimensionality of the configuration.

An important distinction regarding dimensionality is that there is absolutely no need for the dimensions of the configuration to correspond to the x and y axes. The location of the dimensions can be rotated in any direction because the configuration is based on the distances between points, not the distances from the points to the dimensions. Even if there is an apparent interpretation that can be made using the x and y axes, the researcher must examine all possible dimensions and select the dimensionality that best explains the positioning of the points.

Second, a researcher must be aware that dimensions, which are actually vectors, may not be the best or the only way to interpret positions of points. Neighborhoods or regions of the map may have some relevance.

Selecting the number of dimensions to retain in an MDS configuration is much like choosing the number of factors to retain in a factor analysis.

Researchers must be very cautious not to surmise that the number of dimensions always corresponds to the number of characteristics or attributes involved.

It is also possible that the number of interpretable characteristics may be less than the dimensionality of the configuration. A researcher may not be able to interpret all of the dimensions in a configuration. For example, in a three-dimensional solution, a researcher may only find one or two dimensions that explain the positions of the points.

Stress is very helpful in determining the dimensionality of a configuration. As a goodness-of-fit measure, stress indicates the appropriateness of a configuration in representing the data. Stress normally decreases as the number of dimensions increases. The researcher's trade-off is that a reduction in the number of dimensions improves interpretability but also increases stress. Normally low stress values indicate a good configuration. However, MDS is prone to "degeneracy," which occurs when the stress minimization process stops at a local minimum which does not correspond to the global minimum of stress for a certain configuration. When this occurs, a low stress measure is reached in a configuration that does not adequately represent the original relationships. In situations where visual inspection is not sufficient for revealing interpretations of dimensions, statistical procedures including multiple regression and canonical correlation can be used.

In a technique known as "embedding property vectors into the space" a researcher can determine a dimension's interpretation by fitting a vector among a set of points. Using multiple regression, an attribute vector which represents a certain characteristic (interpretation) can be tested as a dimension.

An expansion of the multiple regression procedure for fitting a vector is the use of canonical correlation analysis to simultaneously fit a set of vectors in space. Canonical correlation analysis seeks to determine the linear association between two sets. In this case, one set is the ratings of each stimulus on the various adjective scales (vectors), while the other set is the values of each stimulus on each dimension in derived space.

Two-dimensional configurations are much easier to use than higher-dimensional configurations and are, therefore, frequently preferred. Higher-dimensional configurations are likely to be useful only when supplementary techniques such as multiple regression and canonical correlation are used to find interpretable solutions. As was mentioned at the onset of this section, interpretations need not be dimensions (vectors). Curves, planes, and clusters can serve as interpretations of an MDS output. Consequently, it is often preferable to have a two- or three-dimensional configuration, where such relations can be discerned, in addition to a higher-dimensional configuration, which has a lower stress.

An additional benefit of a two-dimensional solution is that it is usually more easily communicated to most audiences than higher-dimensional configurations that cannot be visualized.

Limitations of Nonmetric MDS

MDS is a relatively new analytic technique. Like most newly developed techniques, as well as some older methods, it is plagued with its share of problems.

A primary problem with MDS procedures is degeneracy of solutions. In some instances, MDS configurations can be markedly changed without the rank order of the interpoint distances being affected. As illustrated in a prior section, a meaningless solution can result if a local minimum is reached despite the existence of a low stress value. Another example of a meaningless solution occurs in preference MDS when all subjects prefer one particular stimuli. While these problems can be resolved by certain procedures, their existence taints the cleanliness of MDS.

Another problem deals with the robustness of MDS solutions to "noisy" data. Collection of proximity and preference data is often influenced by such factors as the nature of the stimuli, the physical environment, and the like. One possible solution to this problem is the use of sensitivity analysis where a researcher attempts to determine how sensitive the configuration is to changes in the data.

Associated with this problem is the issue of statistical inference. The question arises as to when an MDS solution is statistically significant. Because of the need to subjectively interpret the MDS output, tests of statistical significance do not lend themselves to MDS.

A major concern of researchers using MDS, which has already been discussed, is the labeling of the dimensions. This stage is highly subjective and it is not difficult for a researcher to be led astray. A particular problem occurs when a researcher insists on finding some explanation for the relative positions of the points when in fact there may be no discernible solution.

Another problem concerns the homogeneity of perceptions over subjects and the related problem of constructing perceptual maps by aggregating data over individuals. Aggregation involves the substitution of averages for individual maps and therefore sacrifices some of the strength of the input data.

A final empirical problem is that of relating perceptual and preference mappings to actual variables in real life. For example, how would a researcher measure the impact of an alteration in a product attribute? Since MDS output is a certain configuration, it is not easily manipulated to test individual elements such as a product attribute or price. A significant shortcoming of MDS is its inability to transform psychological dimensions into some manipulatable dimension. MDS procedures are inadequate for generating or testing new product ideas or ideas that involve new dimensions.

As such, it would appear that MDS models are more diagnostic than prescriptive.

Fundamental problems still exist in behavioral research regarding the terms *similarity* and *preference*. It has been shown through psychological experimentation that different subjects adapt different strategies in assessing similarity. The criteria by which similarity judgments are made may interact with the stimuli. These problems relate directly to the specific type of data that are required for MDS. MDS is not a tool that can simply be applied to an existing set of data—say, for example, collected in a field survey. Rather, MDS requires specific types of input data that often necessitate individual data collection procedures for a particular study.

A second conceptual problem concerns how subjects derive an overall similarity or preference ratings of stimuli. Little is known about how subjects combine differences in stimulus pairs over several dimensions to come up with overall similarity or preference judgments. There is the possibility that, in an attempt to simplify the comparison process, subjects will evaluate stimuli on one simple criterion rather than consider the numerous attributes of the stimuli.

Applications of MDS

In its short lifetime, MDS has been utilized in a multitude of areas that vary both in content and purpose. This section will highlight the major areas in which MDS has been used (Cooper, 1983).

Marketing applications of MDS are quite varied. The general classifications in which applications will be presented are product planning and market segmentation, distribution channels, personal selling and advertising, and pricing.

A major use of MDS in marketing has been in planning strategies for new and existing products. Perception and preference mapping have been applied to a wide variety of product classes (beer, soft drinks, cars, cereals, fabric softeners, transportation modes, and antacids, among others). Typically, product planning uses of MDS tend to answer questions such as "what are the major evaluative dimensions of a product class?" or "what existing brands are perceived to be similar to what other existing brands?"

By mapping proximity or preference data for products or brands, a researcher can draw conclusions about how consumers perceive products relative to other products and relative to certain attributes. This helps managers develop (re)positioning strategies (Shocker and Srinivasan, 1974; Donthu and Rust, 1988; Rust and Donthu, 1988).

A second product planning area where MDS has been applied is market segmentation. A product class and its buyers can be represented in a joint space where dimensions represent product characteristics, stimulus points represent brands, and ideal points represent buyers. A market segment can be viewed as a subspace of such a configuration. Using MDS, market segments can be constructed based on perceptions of a set of subjects rather than, or in addition to, the demographic, geographic, or product usage characteristics normally used to segment markets. If an MDS configuration produced a subspace with many ideal points but few stimuli (products), a marketer could conceivably find an unfilled market segment (Green and Wind, 1973).

Wind (1978) focused on the groupings of customers rather than the positioning of products, and showed that the same product may require different packaging, promotion, pricing, and distribution to attract different consumer segments.

MDS has been heavily used in developing new product models. Srinivasan and Shocker (1973) suggested nonmetric MDS of similarities to allow consumers to generate a market definition. MDS has also been used to discover relevant attributes for products using similarities questions. Further, MDS has been used to create perceptual product spaces and to model individual or consumer segment decision making.

MDS studies of distribution have dealt mainly with the relations among different retail outlets. Mackay and Olshavsky (1975) studied the differences between cognitive maps of retail locations based on MDS of proximity judgments and found that MDS maps relate to preferences and actual shopping behavior.

An MDS application to personal selling was done by Turner (1971) who inferred the number and kinds of criteria that individual salesmen used in evaluating their customers. In advertising, MDS has been used to track the effectiveness of repositioning or changing a brand name.

A second area of advertising research deals with the compatibility of attributes or slogans with the perceptual image of a brand. MDS has also been utilized to understand the impact of pricing on brand perceptions. Ryans (1974) used nonmetric MDS to represent perceived characteristics of durable goods. He then used the utility function and price to predict the rank order preferences for a new product among a set of 12 products. Hauser and Simmie (1981) studied the joint effect of budgets and preferences in consumer choice. Perceptual maps were developed such that attributes of analgesics—efficacy and gentleness—were transformed into efficacy per dollar and gentleness per dollar.

An overview of MDS applications in one particular field could give the misleading impression that MDS is exclusively used in a marketing context. MDS is used in virtually all social sciences that deal exclusively with nonmetric data. Listed below are some examples of how MDS has been utilized in other research disciplines.

Political scientists have used MDS to map perceptions of political candidates and determine why candidates are perceived as being similar or dissimilar. Anthropologists have used MDS to study cultural differences of various groups based on beliefs, language, and artifact information. Urban and regional planners have identified similarities and dissimilarities of various cities, towns, counties, or regions in terms of a reduced configuration derived from a set of demographic, economic, and financial factors.

Psychologists have used MDS to understand perceptions and evaluations of such things as speech, colors, and personality. And sociologists have used MDS to determine the structure of a group based upon interpersonal perceptual and behavioral differences.

Outlook for MDS

MDS has evolved through a period in which it was first embraced by researchers and then was criticized for not meeting its early expectations. At this stage in its development, MDS has been quite thoroughly analyzed, tested, and applied and has achieved respectability among analytic techniques.

To be sure, there are many fronts yet to be explored in the use of MDS. The combination of MDS with other consumer-based measurement techniques represents a fertile research area. In an applied sense, MDS needs to be further developed as a tool for analyzing new products in new markets rather than being limited to diagnostic procedures in existing markets. As long as MDS is not expected to be a panacea to all research needs, it should continue to be a powerful and valuable methodology in marketing and advertising.

4

Discussion on Chapter 3

Robert Maxwell and David Poltrack
with response by Roland Rust and Naveen Donthu

Comments by Robert Maxwell (Home Box Office)

As you know, pay television is not involved in the advertising business, but we do have a good perspective on the cable business. The authors are bullish, as are others, on the future of cable. The authors also feel that cable's future will be in narrowcasting or delivering niche services to consumers—services that can be marketed and programmed to meet selected consumer tastes. In a sense, the authors are suggesting that cable services, if correctly positioned, can increasingly steal more audience from commercial television and implicitly increase cable penetration and retention.

While I am spiritually in agreement with the article, and applaud the efforts to help the cable business, I really don't think the issue is one of creating or refining more program services, but is more fundamental—that is, in understanding the positioning of cable in home entertainment.

The growth of the cable business has been driven up to now by the consumer's desire to get better reception and the added choice provided by the segmented services that cable provides. I think those consumer benefits have carried the business as far as they can. Consequently, I don't have much to say about the methodology offered in chapter 3. I think it's fine; I'm not sure I understand it. What is said seems to be true: new program services can be created and old program services refined using the technique.

However, I really don't think more niche services are what the cable industry needs today. The business needs to solve two issues: (1) How to increase penetration of cable, and (2) How to reduce churn.

My feeling is that more programming services will not affect these very much. However, a significant increase in the volume of new, quality programming similar to what the networks produce would probably make a difference, and that means broad appeal programming, not niche services. I agree with David Poltrack: what works on cable is broad appeal programming, but I don't think that's in the cards for the business, at least not today. I do think what is needed is an assessment—call it research— into cable's role or positioning in home entertainment, in order to determine what other inherent benefits cable can deliver that would create greater demand for cable and ensure greater loyalty.

Demand and loyalty are two factors which would increase penetration and retention and, importantly, cut down on the current high cost associated with maintaining a subscriber base. To illustrate this point, I'd like to comment on the issues of penetration and retention and suggest that more program services aren't what we need. Instead, a way to understand and position cable's role in home entertainment is needed so that we can grow the business beyond its present level.

It might be helpful to give you some background on the cable business and how it works. I'll use my business, pay television, as an example. There are two key points. First, HBO is distributed to about 4,000 affiliates or cable systems throughout the country; they are our retailers and we, like any manufacturer, are in many cases only as good as our retailer. They, in effect, have more to say about the positioning of our product than we do. This is also true for the basic services such as USA and MTV. The second point—and it's an important one—is that the cable and pay business is not a steady state business. It is a highly transactional business with consumers entering and leaving the category at a fairly rapid rate. They have to make a conscious decision to pay for us every month. For example, transactions due to people (or subscribers) moving is 20% a year. And that's just one reason why people disconnect. The point is that in order to maintain the same subscriber base, pay services and cable companies constantly have to replenish an enormously leaky bucket, by constantly reconnecting old subscribers and getting new subscribers to sign up. It's expensive to roll the trucks, so to speak.

However, despite these enormous transactions, according to research at HBO, consumers are increasingly telling us that they treat pay and cable as a utility, which is to say that they pay their bill in somewhat the same frame of mind that they pay Con Ed or the phone company. Now that seems to be a good place to be.

At the same time, these consumers do disconnect us—they don't disconnect Con Ed or the phone company or if they do, they reconnect on their own initiative—so that unlike the utilities the cable business has to market them back. That tells me that maybe consumers want to treat us like a utility but we're not quite giving them that something extra which will allow their full-fledged treatment of us as a utility. And if cable can increasingly position itself with utility features so that subscribers come to us, it would greatly reduce the high cost of marketing to refill the leaky bucket.

I don't think that's going to happen by adding more or better services. I think it has to do with the fundamental positioning of cable in home entertainment relative to commercial television, VCRs, etc. What is cable and what are its unanswered possibilities in home entertainment? Those are the key questions. Again, I think cable's attributes of reception and choice have carried it this far; but something new is needed to give it full-fledged utility status. By looking at the current problems we face with penetration and retention, this becomes more of an imperative.

Penetration

Let me turn now to the penetration of households. Increasingly it is fundamental to the growth of the business. Currently, cable reaches almost 50% of U.S. households. And it has accomplished this in roughly 15 years. Everyone praises this development and expects continued growth. However, there are other questions that we need to address. One is, why do we assume that cable will continue to grow? For example, in 1980 it grew 30%, in 1981 47%, but in 1982 it dropped to 22%.... In 1986 the penetration increase was only 6%. Penetration is starting to slow.

Another question is: where is the growth coming from? It seems that a good portion of growth is continuing to come from increased distribution into unwired areas. For example, in 1980, 35 million homes were passed by cable and today it's 68 million. However, while cable penetration is increasing nationally—as more consumers have it available—those who have *not* bought the product are still *not* buying it. Currently, while 42 million American households have bought cable, 26 million have said no. And according to our figures, 75% of these express no intention to buy regardless of what kind of service is offered. That's a large, resistant group.

A third question is: why are consumers rejecting cable? The reasons are simple—it has to do with cost and consumer satisfaction with traditional TV. The reverse side of this is that reception and added choice don't create enough demand to drive consumers to us. Certainly one way to increase penetration is to drop price—but that's hard for the operator to do. Also, these rejectors tend to be older and to have lower incomes. It's not surprising that these consumers tend to be very price-resistant. After all, the monthly cost of cable alone is, on the average, about $20 a month. That's over $200 a year, and for many consumers that's a major expenditure.

Well, why is increased penetration so important to cable? It's important for the simple fact that ad-supported cable services are at a structural disadvantage with commercial television which has access to nearly 100%

of U.S. households. While cable is in nearly half of U.S. households, someone like the Fox network can come along and access 80% overnight. The more households a network has access to, the more valuable are its ratings. Right now television ratings aren't equal between cable services and the networks. A five rating on CBS translates into 4.4 million households, since CBS reaches 100% of U.S. TV households. On the other hand, a five rating on the USA cable channel, for example, reaches only 1.7 million households, because USA only has access to 38% of U.S. households. One way the cable advertising supported services can help penetration—and retention—is to get better programs to get more viewing; but first they need better ratings—call it revenue—to be able to buy the programs. It's a chicken or egg dilemma. However, a clear task for the services and for the cable operator should be to expand penetration so these services can offer the same type of household delivery offered by the big guys—ABC, CBS, and NBC.

The final question is, how can cable increase penetration? I think there are three ways.

The first is to create new services; but I think the upside here is limited. For example, at HBO we've created a service called "Festival" which is perfectly positioned against the current content resistor. We will increase cable penetration, but not by much, and it will be a tough marketing sell. Thus I don't think there are many more program services ideas out there that will drive penetration deeper.

The second way to help increase penetration is by promoting and advertising what exists now. Typically, a cable system will spend about 10% of its revenues on promotion. However, in a heavily transactional business where subscribers are constantly leaving and entering the category—which is the reality of the cable and pay television business—it is necessary to spend about 25% of revenues on promotion. That's about what it is in another highly transactional business: magazines. Also, cable advertising–supported services have to realize they are not just program services, but marketers too.

If you believe the research of Paul Kagan, over the last quarter of this year HBO has added over a half million subscribers—no small feat at a time when critics had been saying pay television was dead. What we did was go out and beat the bushes to get new installs through premiums, offers, widgets, free installs, and generally aggressive and smart marketing. It's not as pretty as positioning research, but it's effective. However, it's a costly endeavor.

Thus penetration gains can be made through marketing—albeit expensively. Enhanced services might help more, but I'm not sure it's going to be enough; I think we have to develop other benefits related to cable, to create demand for the product.

So a third way to increase penetration is to develop cable benefits beyond reception and niche services—benefits that will create greater demand and cement loyalty so that cable can adopt the utility status consumers seem to be willing to give us. I'll discuss some ideas later.

Retention

Thus far I have discussed how to increase penetration. The second major issue is retention—keeping subscribers. I'll be brief here, because in a transactional business the discussion about penetration and retention are somewhat related.

Currently, the yearly disconnect rate for pay TV is over 40%. It's about 30% for basic services. That means that yearly there are many subscribers needed to replace, not only to grow the business but just to stay the same. We not only have to sell new subscribers; we have to reconnect old ones.

There are many reasons for consumers leaving the category: people are dissatisfied with the product; they can't afford it; they move; or they don't use it enough. Fortunately, we're seeing a decline in the disconnect rate and an increase in the amount of subscribers who have had HBO for several years. In a sense it's a validation of the utility status I've mentioned.

However, many in the cable business say that it's a fact of life that our business is transactional like the magazine business, and that we'll always have to spend on marketing—and it's a steep cost. My point is, why should we assume we're like the magazine business? Consumers don't assign utility status to *Time* magazine. As I said earlier, consumers are giving cable and pay utility status, but not utility respect. I think we've got something to learn about consumers perception of cable and its position in home entertainment, relative to other new cable products we might develop and to the competition.

One of the factors affecting retention is usage. This is where the work of Rust and Donthu can be most useful. Currently, while we are seeing viewing of the cable category continue to grow, it is not clear where the growth is coming from. It seems to be primarily due to the increase in new services and the distribution of these services, and not due to a growth in the viewing to individual services. In fact, we are seeing a slowdown in viewing to the basic services.

There are several things that can be done to increase viewing. First, the cable services can be fine-tuned by the methods suggested here to help increase viewing, but I don't think it will make much difference. What is really needed is a great deal of new and fresh programming, and that takes a lot of money; it's probably not in the cards for some time.

However, positioning research can be used to help viewing among light viewers of cable services. In many cases, it's the heavy viewer that drives cable usage. For example, 86% of MTV viewing (by those who view for an hour or more a week) is accounted for by 21% of the audience. What seems to be needed is a way to develop programming to expand viewing among this large body of light viewers—which will help overall ratings. Cable services must broaden their appeal, not become more segmented.

The second way to increase viewing is promotion. The ad-supported services offer a lot of programming, but they need to promote their own product to develop habitual viewing, which in turn will help to create loyalty. The cable consumer now gets 1600 hours of ad-supported programming a week and watches about eight. That's over 400 hours a year. At the same time, the average basic cable bill is about $200 a year—that's $.50 an hour for viewing. That's pretty cheap entertainment, but the consumers still don't think it's a good value. Something's missing.

Summary

In summary, I think positioning research can be helpful in expanding viewing among light users of cable's existing services, but what is really needed is a massive amount of money to spend on programming. That's not going to happen right away. However, I feel that the real issue is to understand cable's role in home entertainment, so that more consumer benefits can be created that will provide inherent consumer demand and loyalty. This will give the consumers a greater reason to treat us as an irreplaceble utility. The cable business is faced with two key challenges: to increase penetration and to increase retention; and it must cut down the high cost of marketing associated with these activities. I'm not sure that that can be done by adding more services or more refined services.

Cable is still a new medium. It has, however, adopted many of the traditions and formats of the older medium—commercial television. I'm not sure that's right. I think cable has to find other consumer benefits that are inherent in the technology and are indispensable to the household, as television is today. I'm not sure what they might be, but I'll raise some possibilities.

First, what about cable's natural ability to be more local than local television? When people are asked what they wouldn't give up in their household, they say the TV set and the refrigerator. That TV set represents commercial television, which represents a connection to the world—both nationally and locally. Maybe cable can take that principle one step further. First, we had national TV news, then local news, now maybe it's time for local local news. Cable has a unique local franchise.

Second, what about regional interconnects? It's another form of localism, and commercial TV can't do that.

Third, are we really exploring the best way cable can work with advertisers in the marketing process? The success of shopping channels and direct response has shown that something is going on with cable as a marketing vehicle.

Fourth, what is the relationship between cable and pay and the VCR? As you know, there is high penetration of VCRs in cable homes. Is there some sort of natural marriage that can take place in the convergence of the two technologies—the VCR and cable? This could be a business waiting to happen.

Fifth, and this is addressed to the cable advertising business, let's treat the cable buy as a package—not as individual services competing for limited dollars.

Finally, the cable services could band together and create a fourth network with blockbuster programming; this would obviously help demand, but it probably won't happen.

This is the kind of thinking—call it research—that I feel will help overcome cable's current problem of limited penetration and high transaction. Also, it represents an opportunity to use positioning techniques, such as those developed by Rust and Donthu, to understand the position of cable in home entertainment and uncover needs not being met. Penetration and retention have gone as far as they can under cable's current consumer benefits of better reception and niche services.

It seems that the cable challenge today is not to develop new program services but to instill new, nonprogramming benefits into cable which make it indispensible in the household; this would cut down on the high cost of transactions in the business and increase penetration.

Consumers are indicating that they are ready to give cable the loyalty implicit in utility status—but they still withhold the respect. That seems to be our task.

Comments by David Poltrack (CBS Broadcast Group)

I have interpreted my role as that of an industry practitioner commenting on the feasibility of the practical application of the evaluation system outlined by Dr. Rust and Dr. Donthu. I have made that interpretation because, while I am familiar with perceptual mapping and some of the mathematical theory behind it, I certainly do not have the technical expertise to critique or even discuss the model itself. However, at CBS, we have experimented with the application of similar approaches and I, therefore, hope that I can provide the authors and the audience with some practical considerations.

Network Share Projections

Before I begin I must take exception to some of the statistics provided in the introduction to chapter 3. The cable penetration figures seem to be on target. An updated 1986 cable penetration figure would be between 47% and 48%.

It is the three-network share figures to which I take exception. The 91% network share in 1977 was an in-season prime-time share. The 72% 1985 share figure is a mystery to me. The in-season network prime-time share for the 1984–85 season was 77 and the three-network 1985–86 season share was 76. Even if the base of measurement is changed to the 52-week calendar year share, the correct figure should be 73. For the record, the CBS projected share for the three networks during the 1989–90 prime-time season is 73% and for the full 1990 calendar year it is 70%, significantly higher than the 61% given. I could spend the rest of the chapter challenging that doomsday scenario for network television, but that is not our purpose.

Now let me focus on the subject at hand.

The Model

Just as the most expensive, finely tuned engine's performance is highly dependent upon the fuel used to run that engine, it would appear to me that this impressive and elaborate model's value will ultimately be more dependent upon the quality of the input than on its mechanics. The question boils down to whether or not we will ultimately end up in the proverbial "garbage in–garbage out" situation.

One immediate danger sign is the share configuration for the 14 cable channels shown in table 3.1. Acknowledging the caveats provided concerning these shares, it is still alarming that they are so out of balance with any existing cable television viewing patterns. WTBS, the leading basic cable service, has one of the lowest reported shares, lower than the Arts and Entertainment and the Disney Channel—an odd pattern for what I assumed was a sample of adults age 18 + . Lifetime, one of the least-watched cable channels, is shown as the leading basic cable service.

I mention these discrepancies not because they, in themselves, invalidate the approach—I accept the caveat given—but because they may be symptoms of a more fundamental underlying problem.

As I understand the model's input, it consists of a listing by respondents of four of their favorite network and public television programs, and a ranking by these same respondents of fourteen cable television channels on a five-point scale.

I therefore assume that critical to the accuracy of the model is the accuracy of these two responses as measures of the respondents' historical and future viewing patterns.

We at CBS have invested a great deal of time, effort, and money attempting to develop the research instruments that accurately reflect viewers' actual as opposed to stated viewing preferences. We have not yet effectively wiped out our major nemesis, the socially desirable response. Viewers will list news programs, programs with any perceived intellectual or cultural aura, and warm, sentimental family programs far out of proportion to the share of actual viewing accounted for by these programs. As I examine the estimated market shares for the established cable services given in table 3.1, I suspect that this nemesis has struck once again. The cable services for which the reported shares seem unrealistically high are Arts and Entertainment (high on the cultural/intellectual scale), and Disney (high on the warm, sentimental, family program scale). The pure entertainment channels, WTBS and USA, have share levels well below expectations. If viewers' reported program preferences do not match real viewing activity, the model's results, no matter how sophisticated its processing operation, are likely to be misleading.

Another shortcoming of the model, a shortcoming compounded by the just-discussed socially desirable response phenomenon, is the interpretation of the results once they have been processed. In the test case given, the new channel was positioned in a location close to the following programs: "60 Minutes," "Nightline," "Magnum P.I.," "Mike Hammer," and "Murder, She Wrote." The authors interpret this co-location of this ideal channel and these programs as suggesting that a channel associated with investigative news reporting programs or action/mystery shows might be called for.

I am immediately suspicious when I see "60 Minutes" and "Nightline" on a favorite program list. "Murder, She Wrote" may be co-located with "60 Minutes" because it follows it on Sunday night, as opposed to being on the list because mysteries are a favored form of television programming among this group of viewers. "Magnum, P.I." and "Mike Hammer" certainly seem to fit into the same program category; however, that makes four out of the five programs mentioned CBS-TV programs, suggesting a possible network bias.

As I was trying to develop a composite profile of the viewer that might find his or her ideal program location in this territory I immediately made one assumption: a light television viewer. All these programs do particularly well with light television viewers. This, in turn, brought to mind one other shortcoming of the model—its failure to weight viewer choice by the volume of viewing represented by each viewer. Certainly an ideal point region inhabited by heavy viewers has more potential than one inhabited by light viewers.

Turning back to the shares shown in table 3.1, one channel for whom the reported share is much higher than experience would support is MTV. We know that MTV is watched primarily by the 18–24-year-old group, a group notorious for its low overall viewing activity. The MTV case introduces another aspect of input error. Regardless of overall viewing activity, just how much of the viewer's stated programming of choice does that viewer wish to include in his or her overall viewing diet? I love ice cream, but I certainly do not want a diet consisting of nothing but ice cream. Likewise, the viewer seeks out diversity on his or her viewing menu. Just about everyone loves "The Bill Cosby Show," but I doubt that anyone would elect to fill their full 20-hours-plus weekly viewing menu with this one show. I believe that this gets to the heart of the problem of turning what is a sound theoretical and operational model into a practical, applied model. Let me provide an example using our unfortunate experience with CBS Cable channel.

The CBS Cable channel was designed to serve those viewers that loved the arts with its variety of music, dance, theatre, film, and commentary. We knew going in that all research results would have to be discounted due to the socially desirable response phenomenon. Indeed, if we had taken our findings literally we might have assumed that CBS Cable, not NBC, would be on top of the ratings race today. However, we felt that we did effectively isolate those viewers that were likely to be true CBS Cable followers.

It was also immediately apparent to us that these viewers did not view a lot of television. While we might have surmised that this would limit the potential audience of CBS Cable, we instead assumed, as the authors' model does, that this light viewing level was at least partially attributable to the lack of the type of programming that appealed to this audience segment on the given alternative channels. Therefore, when CBS Cable was available, their viewing would increase. We were probably right to some extent, but we overestimated the degree of the increased viewing.

The fact is that no matter how much someone likes opera they are only going to spend a certain amount of their day listening to it or, in this case, watching it. What we discovered is that the more selective a program category is, the more limited is not only the percentage of the population attracted to it but also the amount of time they are willing to devote to it. In the case of CBS Cable, this limiting situation was fortified by the fact that those viewers most likely to be drawn to CBS Cable were active, involved people with a relatively scarce supply of leisure time.

As a result of these dynamics, the viewing levels achieved by CBS Cable fell below expectations. We were accurate in our projections of the weekly reach of the channel, but overly optimistic in our projections of the frequency of viewing of the channel by its supporters.

Learning from this experience, and faced with the decision whether or not to close down the channel, I half-facetiously suggested that we convert it to a pay channel. The high social desirability index of the service would make it a prestige purchase and our revenue stream would, therefore, be tied to the perceived benefit of having the channel as opposed to being tied to the actual viewing of the channel.

I would like to pause for a moment to make what I believe to be a critical point having to do with the potential success of a cable channel. Cable television continues to be associated with narrowcasting. However, to date, the most successful cable channels have not been narrowcast services at all, with the exception of MTV. I would put WTBS, USA, ESPN, CNN and CBN in the category of broadcast-derivative services.

To me a narrowcast service is defined as one that targets a particular narrow segment of the viewing population and then provides a unique form of programming for that segment. MTV, therefore, meets the narrowcast definition. Its programming form is unique. All of these other services provide program forms that can be found on network and independent broadcast schedule.

ESPN and CNN do not provide narrowcast services. They fail to meet both qualifications. They do not target their programming to a narrow audience segment. The fans of televised sports represent a significant majority of American men and many women and children as well. Almost all U.S. adults watch some televised news programming.

Both of these services have come to be critically evaluated not by the uniqueness of their programming, but by how close they come to the quality of the network sports and news programming. They are derivative services providing a full diet of a form of programming already available on a limited basis on network television. They do not offer the viewers anything new; they offer them freedom from time constraints in viewing a form of programming that was, in the past, limited to certain times of the week or day.

This digression was necessary to set up my next point regarding the practical application of the Rust-Donthu model.

Assuming that the model correctly identifies an unfilled programming hole, how then does the cable entrepreneur fill that hole?

Let's return to the CBS Cable example. Having isolated a programming hole—an arts-based channel—CBS began to attempt to develop the programming to fill that hole. What CBS found was that the viewers they were seeking to attract were among the most discriminating. They were not willing to accept anything but the finest in program content; they knew good from bad when it came to their areas of interest. But they were also discriminating in another way. They had come to expect a certain level of production quality—the production quality they had experienced on network television. They expect this quality on CBS Cable as well.

It was rather obvious that if CBS Cable were to serve a narrow segment of the viewing audience with unique programming of network television quality, a significant revenue stream would have had to be developed. This was not possible and CBS Cable closed shop.

Arts and Entertainment has taken a different approach. This channel relies heavily on foreign product. Government-controlled television in Europe and Japan has subsidized the production of high-quality arts programming. Arts and Entertainment imports this programming, reducing significantly the pressure to produce its own high-quality programming. With this lower cost base, Arts and Entertainment may make it, despite its low viewing levels. The point is that isolating a programming hole is not the major problem, filling that hole is the major problem.

Conclusion

In conclusion I feel that Dr. Rust and Dr. Donthu have developed an impressive framework for evaluating viewer preferences. The challenge now is to develop the fuel that will allow this finely-tuned engine to perform at full capacity. My own recommendation would be to explore the utilization of the huge Nielsen or Arbitron local market sweeps data banks (over 100,000 diaries per sweep) as a possible source of more objective, richer viewing preference data—data that would be free of the distortions of the socially desirable response, and that would allow for weighting of viewers by level of viewing.

Response by Roland Rust and Naveen Donthu

David Poltrack's experiences with CBS Cable give him a unique perspective on the practical difficulties of successfully implementing a new cable network. While we agree with most of Mr. Poltrack's comments, there are some issues that we would like to address further.

Data Quality

The metaphor of a fine-tuned engine needing high-quality fuel seems apt. We would therefore explain more completely how we can ensure a reasonable octane level. In our case, this means making sure our viewership data truly represent the population.

First, what happens if the data are unrepresentative? As Mr. Poltrack points out, there are several potential pitfalls. The data collection method, relying on self-report of favorite networks and programs, will hardly compete with meters (or diaries) as a ratings method. It does not even attempt to measure viewing, which makes the validity of its ratings estimates highly suspect.

There is also the problem of the socially desirable response, in which respondents purport to prefer highbrow programming. Also, some respondents are light viewers, often the same ones who prefer the most intelligent and artistic programs.

Our response to all of the above problems is the same: reweight the data to conform to objective viewing data sources, or (as Mr. Poltrack suggests) use the objective viewing data directly. Direct use of people meter data would clearly solve the above problems, but would require concurrent network viewing and specific cable channel viewing data, which are not currently readily obtainable. Use of diary data, in addition to the availability problem, leaves the researcher vulnerable to the socially desirable response.

We therefore recommend using meter data as a ratings standard and reweighting the respondents such that our projected ratings match the published figures. This procedure has already been employed in a radio station positioning model (Donthu, Rust, and Lynch 1987). The reweighting procedure (which is outlined in the above paper) will have two main consequences. Light viewers will tend to be weighted less, and ratings projections based on the model will tend to be more accurate. It is also possible to weight the respondents according to disposable income, membership in particular target market, or any other measurable respondent criterion.

Multiple Ideal Points

The most troublesome issue noted by Mr. Poltrack was that an individual may not be characterized accurately by a single ideal point. He points out that even an opera buff would not wish to watch opera all the time. To some extent this objection is met by the reweighting scheme (such opera buffs would receive less weight) and the dispersion of ideal points. However, extensive variety seeing would present undeniable difficulties for our model. One possible solution would be to allow an individual to have multiple ideal points, which is more difficult to model.

Narrowcasting vs. Broadcasting

The issue of narrowcasting also deserves mention. Some speakers at this conference have suggested that the most successful cable networks do not narrowcast. This assertion may result from too narrow a view of narrowcasting, based on too narrow a view of segmentation. Mr. Poltrack, for example, states that ESPN and CNN are not narrowcasters, because they do not program to a narrow audience segment. The target segments are instead considered broad, because large numbers of people watch some sports or some news.

While we may disagree on semantics, his view is actually compatible with our model, which assumes that a cable network's audience share is derived not just from those individuals for which the network is ideal, but also to varying degrees from those who prefer other kinds of programming. Thus ESPN may narrowcast to sports nuts while realizing that a significant part of its audience will come from people who are less fanatic. An advantage of our model is that it can project ratings using both kinds of viewers. In the ESPN case, the sports nut will be estimated to have a higher probability of choosing ESPN than the nonsports nut, but the projected rating will involve a weighted average of both types of viewers.

Part II

Implications for Advertising

5

The Television Viewing Environment: Implications of Audience Change

Dean M. Krugman

Introduction

It is clear that the viewing environment of today is substantially different from that of the 1960s and 1970s. At times we forget that television, as we know it, is a relatively new phenomenon in American life. Change should be expected.

The number of television stations and viewers grew rapidly from 1952 to 1964. From 1964 to 1976 we saw color, a rapid increase in multiple sets, dominance by the networks, and an era of enormous growth in broadcast advertising. The year 1976 introduced satellite distribution, the initial major growth of cable and the introduction of a successful pay-service HBO. Even with those changes, the 1965–1980 era was an extremely stable one that is not likely to come again.

As planners we had been, to a limited degree, stuck in the 1970s with a view of television that accounts for cable but discounts the overall picture of changing audiences and their relationship to television technology. This situation is understandable, because we got "blue skied" in the early 1970s. That is, we were told by academics and practitioners that new technology— particularly cable with its interactive capability—was going to change our lives dramatically. The industry recoiled when major change did not occur in quick order.

Audience change has been slower, but very consistent. We are now realizing that the era with which we are the most familiar (and in many cases grew up in) is gone. To be sure, change in television audiences is a

constant issue with which we must deal. The focus of this chapter is to
overview changing viewing audiences and to provide an analysis of that
change. The scope is limited to the new television services that are viewing-
oriented. Cable, pay cable, pay-per-view (PPV) and videocassette recorders (VCRs) will be considered. Presented initially is an assessment of
each viewing group based on recent academic and industry research. Following this is a conceptualization of how these services fit together, and a
discussion of research issues. Finally, this chapter suggests some implications for advertisers and media planners.

General Trends

There are numerous facts and figures relating to the audiences of television. However, there is little systematic research that investigates audience habits of the past and the present in a consistent fashion. In retrospect,
researchers have not taken advantage of longitudinal techniques to gauge
change.

Only one consistent measure of the television audience had been conducted from 1960 through 1980. This is the survey work of Gary Steiner
in 1960 that was replicated, with modifications, by Robert T. Bower in
1970 and 1980. The original work was spawned by the Bureau of Applied
Social Research at Columbia University. The book from which the following baseline information has been taken was published by Columbia University Press (Bower, 1985).

The amount of time spent with television increased by 20% from 1960
to 1980. The television was reported to be "on" much more often in 1980
than in 1960. Viewers in 1980 had a lower general regard for television
than in previous years, yet had a better regard for the specific programs
watched. That is an interesting contradiction—one which Bower attributes
in part to an increase in viewing options:

> The larger number of programs available (in 1980) to the average viewer
> at any one time would permit him to be more selective in his choices,
> indeed permit him to find more programs that he would find "extremely
> enjoyable" even when it is his impression that the general quality of
> television fare was declining. (Bower, 1985:29)

It is evident that cable distribution has increased the choice of programming. However, we still operate under the assumption that the motivation
for watching and the process of watching are not particularly involving.
This goes back to Bogart (1956) who called television a "pastime." In his
recent work on television audience, Bower (1985) supported this premise
when he concluded that a strong motivation to view, or careful attention
to content, is not usually the case. A more derogatory term of the past is
"boob tube." Today students call television viewing "zoning out." Much

of our industry planning is based on the premise that television selection and viewing is a passive activity.

Some recent research contradicts, in part, the concept of audiences as passive program selectors and viewers. Rubin (1983) found two major motivations for television viewing: (1) ritual viewing based on habit and relaxation, and (2) instrumental viewing based on active participation and information. The latter is more directed. Childers and Krugman (1987) noted that more traditional television audiences were ritualized in their viewing but that individuals who subscribed to a new pay service were instrumental. Commenting on advertising and involvement, Greenwald and Leavitt (1984) observed that "it is part of the popular lore that print is a more involving medium than audio or video" (1984); however, they note that all advertising media are processed at a low level and that we need to explore the ability of a medium to "boost" involvement upward.

In part, audiences of the new media have exhibited different motivations and viewing patterns that can allow for more active, "boosted up" viewing. This suggests that we need to reexamine the motivations for audiences' viewing and for the actual way they view. It is no longer safe to assume that the knowledge generated for the audiences of the 1970s and even early 1980s will hold in today's multichannel, multiservice environment.

Audiences of the New Media

Both practitioners and researchers in this area have continued to call for a greater understanding of the way new viewing relationships have formed as a result of cable, pay cable, PPV, and VCR (Domzol and Kernan, 1983; James, 1983; Levy, 1983; Sparkes, 1983; Krugman, 1985). The following examines audience research on new media services and provides an update on their status.

Nonsubscribers to Cable

There are two kinds of nonsubscribers to cable: (1) those who elect not to subscribe, and (2) those who do not have the opportunity to subscribe.

Forty-four percent of the homes passed by cable elect not to subscribe. Individuals electing not to subscribe tend to be older, have fewer children and lower family incomes (Webster, 1983). Generally, they are satisfied with television as they know it (Banks and Gagnard, 1984). These individuals think "television is television" and do not feel the costs of cable are worth benefits received (Baldwin and McVoy, 1983). They are more reliant on local media (Webster, 1983). The use of radio, newspaper, and local television is greater for this group (Kaplan, 1978).

This group is distinct and can be characterized as more traditional viewers. Conceivably, they fit the category of less active viewers. The group also tends to resist new technologies. They are less venturesome in their attitude and adoption of VCRs and home computers (Dickerson and Gentry, 1983; Rothe, Harvey and Michael, 1982).

Twenty-six percent of the television homes are not passed by a cable system. Two-thirds of the individuals in the top ten markets do not currently have the opportunity to subscribe (Standard and Poors, 1986). Most of these are inner-city markets that have franchises granted or under construction. As these markets come on line, a good deal must be known about who will and will not subscribe to both the basic and pay services. Initially it was felt that many economically disadvantaged groups, who comprise much of the inner-city population, would not subscribe to pay services. This prediction is consistent with the idea that pay services are generally for upscale consumers. However, some early indications show this may not be the case and that pay services provide these groups with an entertainment option at a competitive price. It may not be reasonable to apply what has been learned about cable adoption in midsized markets to the inner-city urban areas.

Basic Cable

Basic subscribers represent 41% of U.S. television homes and 56% of all homes passed. Conservative estimates predict a 54% penetration by 1990 and 64% in the year 2000 (Krugman and Rust, 1987). This is based on a 1% growth per year. While the watershed of 1976 to 1986, where penetration grew from 15% to 41%, is over, there will still be a substantial increase. This increase will affect advertisers and the ability to reach markets. It is important to note that the basic cable group is no longer a homogenous group and will become even more heterogeneous as cable penetration increases.

Basic cable users have younger household heads, more children, and are more affluent and upscale (National Demographics and Lifestyle, 1986). They want more program variety (Becker, Dunwoody, and Raefaeli, 1983; Metzger, 1983), and are not as satisfied with traditional television (Banks and Gagnard, 1984). As expected, they watch less local television (Webster, 1983). Two studies indicate these homes read less (Kaplan, 1978; Rothe, Harvey and Michael, 1982). A portion of this group sees cable as a way to obtain pay services (Krugman and Eckrich, 1982).

Presently, basic cable users are more technically oriented than traditional viewers and exhibit a greater willingness to use new technologies. They are more likely to adopt both VCRs and home computers (Dickerson and Gentry, 1983; Krugman, 1985).

What is most interesting about this group is that they tend to be more active in their motivations for using television. Certainly they are more selection oriented. Segments in this group look for and utilize more channels. However, extended channel use is not evenly dispersed. There is evidence to show that individuals develop distinct repertoires of stations in this multichannel environment (Heeter and Greenberg, 1985).

Webster (1986) studied audience behavior in what was termed "the new viewing environment." He found that audiences used the specialized cable channels very differently than they used the networks or even the superstations distributed by cable. Erosion from the networks was not evenly dispersed, and a high degree of polarization was found in viewing schedules.

Audiences of specialized cable channels such as sports, music, religion, etc., used those channels very frequently. For these specialized channels, a smaller, yet constant, audience base emerged. The superstations, with programming more similar to the networks, displayed a wider, less frequent base. Therefore, a 5% drop in audience from network viewing was not at all evenly dispersed. This development is important because it shows that smaller, more loyal segments are forming for specialized cable channels. To a limited degree they can take on the characteristics of specialized magazines. It allows for some introspection about the way audiences select and view in the multichannel environment. Several questions arise: do audiences of these specialized channels pay more attention to content? Are they more active? What is the opportunity to extend this notion to more specialized advertising messages based on the concept of a more active audience?

Pay Cable Subscribers

Pay cable subscribers represent 25% of the U.S. (60% of the basic cable homes). Because of industry changes brought on by deregulation, this is an audience in flux. Therefore, our current knowledge may not be very useful.

From 1980 to 1985 pay cable users formed a distinct segment. They are characterized as having younger household heads, having more individuals in the home, being more affluent, and viewing slightly more television than cable homes (Baldwin and McVoy, 1983; Rothe, Harvey, and Michael, 1982; Webster, 1983).

Pay users approach television in a different manner. Television is seen as a more important source of entertainment (Krugman and Eckrich, 1982). This group does not appear to be escaping broadcast television; rather they want to enhance their viewing experience. Selection of pay programming is seen as more active than basic cable viewing and much more active than traditional viewing. Pay subscribers tend to be more open to new products and more venturesome (Krugman, 1985). They were also more open to new technologies (Danko and MacLachlan, 1983; Dickerson and Gentry, 1983).

Pay industry subscriptions and revenues have been flat. Price rates are going up for basic and down for pay. Industry observers have noted that basic cable service prices are inelastic and that pay service prices are elastic (Standard and Poors, 1986). Therefore, with prices going down for pay, one would expect some modest growth.

However, increased industry competition is a key concern. Pay audiences can be broken into at least two categories: those that purchase multiple pay services, and those that purchase only one pay service. They are not the same. A study in progress at the University of Minnesota and the University of Georgia (Childers and Krugman, 1987) indicates that the multiple pay group is both more directed to television and more open to technology than the single pay group (see chapter 11). The impact of competition should be different for these groups. This situation is examined in the section of this chapter devoted to competition for viewers.

Pay Per View

Pay per view (PPV) is the newest service to be introduced. In PPV, cable programming is purchased at a single time rather than a schedule of programs. The user must interact with the cable company to specifically order the program. This can be a phone call with a specialized code or a decoder box at the set. While industry data indicate that most orders for PPV programming arrive shortly before the scheduled time, this does not imply that viewers have not "acted" in the process of getting ready to view. By its very nature the antecedent of PPV viewing is more activity.

Industry revenues for PPV were 40 million in 1985 and 78 million in 1987. Projections differ on PPV revenues by 1990. The NCTA project revenues to be 1.1 billion by 1990. Standard and Poors (1986) projects revenues to be between one-half billion and one billion. Obviously, we are coming into a fast growth period. With cable profits maturing and pay cable profits declining, PPV is seen as a major source of future industry revenues.

To date there is little published research on PPV. A recent study (Childers and Krugman, 1987) found that PPV is evaluated in a differential manner depending on the existing television services already being used in the home. The results of that study encompass both pay cable and VCR users and will be reported later in this chapter.

There is some sports PPV programming that is purchased on a package basis. The viewer buys a certain number of games or events. To date, there is little research in this area, but it raises a number of questions about our willingness to pay for select programming. In my estimation, these sports/events packages illustrate a more directed viewing than traditional pay cable but with the opportunity to have commercials readily accepted.

VCR

The rapid diffusion of VCRs has intrigued industry analysts. In 1980 VCRs were in less than 5% of U.S. television homes. By the end of 1987 they will be in a minimum of 40% of U.S. homes. Projections place penetration at 50% by 1990 (Video Forecast, 1985). The rise was so quick that some studies captured only the first-wave "early adopters." Therefore, we must be cautious when projecting the behavior patterns of early adopters to second- and third-wave adopters. While research has told us who buys VCRs, and has identified some basic reasons for use, we know surprisingly little about how this product influences and perhaps changes the viewing process.

Research conducted between 1980 and 1985 indicates that VCR use correlates heavily with cable subscriptions and other in-home technologies such as personal computers (Dickerson and Gentry, 1983; Krugman and Eckrich, 1982; Rothe, Harvey and Michael, 1982). VCR users are portrayed as more technology oriented and utilizing multiple television services. Levy (1981; 1983) concluded that "time shifting," where individuals record to view at a different time, is a major factor. The process of program selection is more control oriented.

National Demographics and Lifestyles (1986) in a large survey of users concluded that the perceived number one VCR benefit was renting and viewing movies at home. The second benefit was time shifting. The study indicates that while movie rental was perceived to be the most important benefit, time shifting was the most frequent activity. This finding is not a contradiction. It is simply easier to time-shift than to shop for movies. Another recent study shows that VCR ownership has indeed influenced viewing patterns. Harvey and Rothe (1986) found that a portion of VCR users reported increased viewing time. More importantly, they found that users felt the VCR increased the "quality" of viewing time.

Both of these benefits—time shifting and movie viewing—point to a more active process in the selection of programming. To a certain degree, they also point to more active viewing of programming.

Zip Zap Flip

Accompanying the VCR is remote control. While the remote control is increasingly popular in regular television set sales, its use has been accentuated by VCRs. Forty-two percent of television homes have remote control (J. Walter Thompson, 1986). Along with the VCR and remote control come three phenomena that have catchy names: zipping, zapping, and flipping.

Zipping is the name given to speeding through commercials previously recorded by VCR. Studies indicate that this phenomenon occurs, but the extent has not been well defined. Yorke and Kitchen (1985) examined zipping in the United Kingdom and found that most individuals did zip through commercials. Another study in the U.S. (J. Walter Thompson, 1986) indicates that zipping takes place in 50% of the homes who have prerecorded programming.

Zapping and flipping are terms used to describe channel switching. Zapping is usually used to describe the behavior associated with avoiding commercials. Flipping is usually associated with program switching. The 1986 study by J. Walter Thompson indicates that flipping occurs 34% of the time and zapping occurs 9% of the time. In my estimation neither is particularly well understood because we have not examined the process of television viewing on an in-depth basis. Most of the work in this area is done by survey research which has a difficult time capturing "how" individuals watch television.

Heeter and Greenberg (1985) note that zappers generally pay less attention to television programming and treat television as an accompaniment to other activities. They argue that in this instance viewing is more passive: "Zappers also consistently tell us they pay less attention to television in general. Furthermore, zappers use television more for background sound than nonzappers, and they more often have the television on without audio" (p. 17).

The above suggests that it is not the technology, the VCR remote control, or television remote control, that influences behavior. Rather, the predisposition already exists, and the technology makes it easier. Greenberg and Heeter were careful not to place zapping as only an advertising issue, but rather, as an issue that must be investigated within the context of total viewing.

Flipping is a factor in the way programs are selected, and different from avoiding commercials. It appears to be a more active process with regard to the way people watch television, and one with more ramifications for programmers than for advertisers. The study by J. Walter Thompson (1986) noted: "The percentage of traditional passive viewers is lower than generally realized. . . . The percentage of impatient dial wanderers-flippers is higher" (p. 11).

Presumably, by "passive viewers," they mean those who watch a program from start to finish. This is a different interpretation from mine, which assumes the motivation to watch and the involvement in watching. However, the J. Walter Thompson conclusion is consistent with the premise that viewers can be more active in both the selection and viewing process. Certainly it points to a competitive viewing environment where viewers have more control.

Competition for Viewing Time

The adoption of more than one new television service has been well documented. Studies have confirmed the adoption, or the desire to adopt, multiple television or telecommunication-oriented technologies. Cable—and, to a larger degree, pay cable users—are more likely to adopt video-cassette recorders and home computers (Rothe, Harvey and Michael, 1982; Harvey and Rothe, 1986; Krugman and Eckrich, 1982; National Demographics and Lifestyles, 1986). Studies primarily focusing on the adoption of home computers note a significant increase in the likelihood of using cable services and videocassette recorders (Dickerson and Gentry, 1983; Danko and MacLachlan, 1983).

The Yankee Group (1986) has noted a group of technologically advanced families (TAF). This segment is predisposed to new technically oriented products such as videocassette recorders, compact disc players, and portable video cameras. This group represents approximately 10% of U.S. homes. This segment is thought to be increasing: "Many of those consumers who last year (1985) dabbled in technology and related products and services have made have made a greater commitment to the use of high technology products and services" (The Yankee Group, 1986).

Having noted the adoption of multiple new television services and products, it would be remiss not to caution that limitations on viewing time exist. A. C. Nielsen (1986) noted at the end of the 1984–85 season that for the first time individual viewing actually declined in the average television household. Viewing is an activity limited by time; only so much can take place. Owning more television equipment does not always translate into viewing more television. While viewing does go up in the homes with cable, pay cable, and VCR units, measuring total household viewing in multi-service homes is somewhat misleading because there are more people in those homes. The much more important criteria is individual viewing.

In addition to the noted erosion of network viewing, increasing competition exists within the new media environment. In 1985–86 we conducted a study to determine the competitive environment of pay cable, PPV, and VCR movie rentals. The purpose was to separately compare PPV with pay cable and VCR rentals (Childers and Krugman, 1987). A number of dimensions were investigated, including product quality, product value, ease of operation, control of viewing, convenience, and perceived similarity.

Individuals who owned a VCR were not as impressed with the PPV service as those who did not own a VCR. It seems likely that VCR users, who have had more exposure to television technology, would be more sensitive to and perhaps more critical of the benefits of a new service. VCRs were rated as more difficult to operate; however, this perception was overcome by the control of viewing time and the program selection.

VCR users were control oriented. They were a more active group, willing to put up with the shopping for movie rentals. This shopping behavior can be observed at any of the thousands of VCR rental outlets around the country. The control- and selection-oriented VCR user will not readily switch over to PPV.

PPV was perceived as more difficult to operate but providing more control than pay cable. The services were rated as equal by customers in terms of the attributes of value and selection. Pay cable subscribers and nonsubscribers did not vary as much in their evaluation of PPV as did VCR owners and nonowners. Using pay cable had not made subscribers more critical of PPV.

Table 5.1 overviews some of these relationships. It illustrates that PPV is a midpoint between pay cable and VCRs. PPV was judged to be much more similar to pay cable than VCR movie rentals. In part I concluded that pay cable was much more vulnerable to PPV than were VCR rentals. Audiences of VCRs liked the control and selection issues. They were more active in the process of deciding what to view. PPV users were active in the process but not as active as VCR users.

Conceptualizing Viewers and the Viewing Environment

Given what we have learned about audiences and the viewing environment, it is now possible to construct an overview of the potential impact new services have on the selection process for viewing and the actual viewing process. Research has established that the motivations for selecting television programming are not always passive and ritualized, and that at times viewers are more directed and active. The actual viewing of programming has been described as passive, with television as accompaniment and background, or more active in terms of attention to content. The processes of selection and actual viewing are distinct: (1) The decision of what to watch, and (2) The actual watching.

Actually, it is probably too dichotomous to note that selection or viewing are either active or passive. Active and passive appear to be at opposite ends of a continuum.

The *decision to watch* is more passive when the viewer is going to watch "something" on television. This is more akin to Rubin's (1983) notion of ritual or habit. The decision to watch is more active when a particular program is viewed and the viewer's schedule is constructed around that program. This same decision can become even more active when the program is time-shifted via a VCR. Shopping for a VCR rental appears to be a very directed effort in the decision to watch. Certainly it requires the viewer to do more in advance.

The *actual watching* of television is something we have not looked at as carefully as we might have with respect to the new television services. Television as background is a passive form of viewing, while close attention to programming is a more active form of viewing. Certain individuals go to great length not to be disturbed during their VCR rentals or pay program. Taking the phone off the hook and going to the movies at home is becoming common. The viewer is more directed toward the television.

Table 5.1
Comparison of Pay PPV and VCRs

	----PAY---- more similar	----PPV---- more different	----VCR----
control of program viewing	little control of schedule	moderate control of schedule	high control of schedule
ease of operation	easy to operate	moderately difficult	more difficult
convenience	very convenient	moderately convenient	less convenient
selection and quality of programs	good selection	good selection	superior selection

This is what is meant by active viewing: the set is the center of the activity, not the background.

New viewing services and technologies have the capacity to change the viewing environment both in terms of control and direction of what is viewed, and the actual attention to what is viewed. The capacity to change the viewing environment focuses on the consequences of having these new services available in the home.

Focus on the consequences of adoption was first argued by Robertson (1971) when he reviewed innovative behavior and communication. Some of the new television services only slightly alter viewing patterns; others require more dramatic changes on the part of the audience. The important factor is the impact new services have on existing consumption patterns. New products requiring only slight or moderate changes are referred to as "continuous" or "dynamically continuous." New products that require a great deal of change are termed "discontinuous."

In a study focusing on the audiences of the new media, I found that the overall scheme of continuous to discontinuous products was supported (Krugman, 1985). Table 5.2 updates that scheme. The scheme looks at the various services and provides a taxonomy based on the capacity to change consumption. As the capacity to alter consumption changes, our existing knowledge of advertising and program viewing becomes less relevant and we need to rethink our assumptions about audiences.

In any viewing situation there is a capacity to be active—that is, to pay close attention to the programming. Not all viewing situations offer the same capacity to control the schedule. There is an implicit assumption that, in some cases of more controlled selection, there is more potential to pay closer attention. This is based on the idea that the viewer has been more active in the process of planning, and that planning activity provides an opportunity for closer attention. The lines are arbitrary and will change as audiences change.

Basic cable services which only slightly alter viewing are characterized as being continuous innovations because consumers are still watching television. The majority of this audience is offered greater selection. This group is more television oriented than traditional viewers who elect not to subscribe. Within this segment, there exist a number of small groups who actively use specialized programming.

Pay cable services bought on a subscription basis are judged to be dynamically continuous. Consumers are now paying for programming without commercial interruptions. At this point viewing has more potential to change in both the planning and actual watching. Less audience flow from program to program is expected; individuals can go to the movies in their home.

PPV requires more active behavior. The viewer must order the pro-

Table 5.2
"Potential" Consumption Changes

	Continuous	Dynamically Continuous	Discontinuous
Traditional Viewing			
Cable	More selection, potential for greater segmentation, can operate on traditional television flow or more directed viewing.		
Pay Cable	Potential for more directed selection and viewing, less audience flow, no commercial breaks.		
Pay-per-view	More directed selection, viewer must "order" program, potential for more directed viewing, more control of viewing schedule. Audience flow not an issue.		
VCR		Much more potential for schedule control in terms of time shifting or renting. Requires more active shopping. Potential for more active viewing. Audience flow not an issue.	
Interactive services, home shopping, banking			Television is performing a vastly different function. It is now an interactive monitor.

gramming. PPV has the potential to assist the viewer in controlling the
schedule. It also has the potential for more directed viewing.

The VCR can be dynamically continuous or discontinuous. Certainly it
allows for more control in terms of "time shifting" regular television programming. However, it also allows planned movie viewing in the home
and requires more shopping behavior in order to obtain the programming.

Interactive services, requiring new forms of behavior, such as home
shopping and banking, are seen as discontinuous because the television set
is performing a vastly different function.

It is important to note that much depends on the existing level of a
product or service within the home. A home with cable and pay cable
service that purchases a VCR is different from a home without cable and
pay cable that purchases a VCR. The consequences of using new television
services are not expected to be the same within homes utilizing different
levels of new television services.

Households adopting new television technologies must be examined
within the framework of the current level of television technology and
services within the home. In proposing an inventory of new diffusion research, Gatignon and Robertson (1985) noted that a major problem has
been our failure to understand the relationship between a new adoption
and the existing consumption system: "Future research could contribute
by focusing on how an innovation fits into the existing consumption system
and inventory patterns" (pp. 854–855).

The PPV results in the last part become much clearer with this perspective. Remember that PPV was rated differently by those who owned
a VCR and those who did not own a VCR. VCR owners were more critical
of the service. Additionally, PPV was not rated as differently by those who
already subscribe to a pay cable service and those who do not. This result
occurred because there is a much greater consumption difference between
the use of VCR and PPV than between pay cable and PPV.

Some Research Issues

The further we move toward discontinuity, the less we can apply our
knowledge of traditional television viewing. Then we need a deeper understanding of the viewing process. The purpose of this paper is to focus
on audience change and not develop a detailed research agenda; however,
it is important to overview the subject. An examination of the literature
indicates that we have spent a good deal of time defining the audiences of
the new media.

Recently Nielsen indicated that people meters will be the sole tool for
1987 ratings. In part this decision is a response to the automated service
introduced by AGB Television Research Inc. Automated devices will help
eliminate a major problem connected with cable viewing: that is, the con-

fusion over the multitude of channels being offered, and the inability of consumers to accurately designate what they are watching. This only solves part of the puzzle. It will tell us who is viewing, but it does little in assessing the quality of viewing. Our overriding concern has been on the questions of: (1) who subscribes to these services? (2) who buys the new technologies? and (3) who is watching or renting?

These questions are most appropriate given that we needed some basic definitions. However, we are in need of answers to at least two more questions: (1) why do people view? and (2) how do people view?

To a limited extent we have investigated the antecedents of viewing by concentrating on motivational research. This investigation has been useful in understanding traditional viewing. However, we need to further our understanding with respect to why individuals select new television services and programming.

To a larger extent, we have not done enough in understanding how people view. It has been demonstrated that the capacity for viewing change is enhanced with the new media services and technologies. If that is the case then we need to examine viewing under these conditions. It is here that advertisers have the best chance to assess the efficacy of both programming and commercial use. This moves us from:

who views $\longrightarrow$ why they view $\longrightarrow$ how they view

A number of other researchers and practitioners have reached this conclusion in their separate areas. Here are a select few:

In researching cable television users' attitudes and behavior, Sparkes concluded in 1983, "The results of attitude measures certainly seem to indicate that public reaction to cable television is a complex one which probably requires numerous different kinds of measures over an extended period of time to map."

Levy published four studies on VCR use and the potential for impact in 1983. He concluded, "New and more sophisticated measurement strategies will be needed to count VCR audiences and understand their behavior."

After investigating television audience segmentation, Domzal and Kernan in 1983 concluded, "The 'new technologies'—cable, STV, VCR, etc.— *require* a rich understanding of audience segmentation since that is the key basis for its efficacy. A distinction, in practical terms, must be made between audience size and satisfaction."

In analyzing the new media for the *Journal of Advertising Research*, James (1983) concluded, "We, as advertisers, need better research, not only do we need better quantitative measurement, we need better qualitative measurement than we may have needed in traditional broadcast television. In addition to knowing more about audience size and composition, we need to know more about viewer 'satisfaction' and 'alternatives'."

In commenting on the use of people meters, David Poltrack (1987), Vice President for Research at CBS, noted, "That brings up a theoretical question, 'What *is* TV viewing?' "

The above are all concerned, in part, with the audience television/new technology relationship. I am urging us to go beyond *who* is viewing, to determine *why* and *how* viewing takes place.

The changing environment demands greater explanation concerning selection and viewing. We need a comprehensive research program to assess the viewer-television relationship. Additionally, program viewing and advertising viewing are not necessarily separate entities. Research must examine advertising viewing within the context of television viewing.

As I have noted, most of the research to date has been conducted via survey methods. Those studies have been helpful but they have not taken us far enough toward understanding new technologies and audience viewing. Methods such as in-home observations and in-depth interview need to be conducted in conjunction with the standard survey approaches. These would greatly increase our understanding.

The research issue takes on far greater significance in terms of young viewers. Many of us grew up in a broadcast television environment that was stable. Our notion of television was networks and independents. When you ask children to talk about television you find a completely different orientation and explanation. The kids of today are reared in a multichannel, more control-oriented environment. A recent Gallup youth survey indicated that the proportion of teens watching movies on the VCR rose dramatically in the past three years from 39% in 1984 to 87% in 1986 (Gallup, 1986). By contrast they went to the theatre 11 times in 1986 compared to 15 times in 1985. To be sure, we need a much stronger understanding of in-home viewing for this group. It has enormous ramifications for the ways in which we attempt to reach changing audiences.

The following are just a few questions that we must answer in helping to determine the audiences of new television services:

1. What is the attention to and use of specialized cable and pay cable programming? Does this differ from traditional viewing?
2. What is the attention level for specialized commercials within specialized programming?
3. What is the capacity for viewing change with time shifting?
4. How do VCR rentals change viewing habits? What is the attention level to VCR rentals?
5. What happens to viewing as different combinations of new television services enter the home? How do we define television viewing?
6. Can we expect the same adoption of cable and pay cable services in inner-city areas that we have in other suburban or mid-sized metropolitan areas?

Researching "how" we view requires a different, more in-depth approach than is used for understanding "who" views. A reasonable starting place is to assess the television viewing environment via in-depth personal and focused interviews. This initial step would help determine the attention we pay to the programming of the different new media services. Following the in-depth interviews, a series of personal in-home interviews and observations could be used to confirm various levels of program viewing.

The end results of this research would be to establish general viewing weights for the different new media services and traditional television viewing. Currently, media planners report the use of various weights in order to purchase advertising (Lancaster, Kreshel, and Harris, 1986). However, little research has been conducted to confirm such a weighting structure.

Finally, the bigger picture of media in society is upon us. While media services do not affect the way we operate, they do impact our social relationships. The rise of in-home entertainment has enormous ramifications for the way we operate. The inner-city dwellers, who now have a more economical entertainment source are rapidly upon us. It is not enough to merely know who they are and what they watch. Rather, we need to better understand how this viewing influences social relationships.

Implications

Recent years have seen a movement away from network viewing and a rise in cable, pay cable, and VCR penetration. Three network prime time shares dropped from 91% in 1976–1977 to 74% in 1985–1986. Cable penetration in that same time period rose from 16% to 42%. Once more, the combined network share is currently 87% in homes not subscribing to cable and 66% for homes subscribing to cable and pay cable.

A recent analysis of viewing trends from 1976 to the present indicates that for every 10% increase in cable penetration there is a 7% decrease in prime time network shares (Krugman and Rust, 1987). This same analysis revealed that for every 10% cable penetration increase there is a 3% drop in network advertising revenues. Presently, the decline in network revenue share is substantially less than the network decline in audience share. While it was concluded that there is a certain inertia towards moving away from previous strategies that call for network programming, the results are ominous when one considers that there is still room for moderate growth in cable penetration.

We have been hearing that cable industry profits are down and that the major growth period in terms of penetration is over. That is only partially true. It behooves us to remember that a modest growth rate at 1% would give cable a 54% penetration by 1990 and a 64% penetration by the year 2000. These are not "blue sky" projections; if anything, the 1990 figure is conservative. (The 54% is a projection of D'Arcy Masius Benton and

Dean M. Krugman

Table 5.3
Projections of Audience and Revenues

	1985	1990(est.)	2000(est.)
Cable Penetration (%)	41.1	54.0	64.0
Network Share of Revenue (%)	91.8	87.5	84.2
Network Share of Audience (%)	72.9	61.7	54.6
Cable Revenue per Cable Household (Divided by the Consumer Price Index)	6/.64	10.31	12.83

Source: Krugman and Rust, Journal of Advertising Research, 1988

Bowles [DMB&B, 1987]. Ronald Kaatz [1985], in *Cable Advertisers Handbook*, estimated a 58%.)

Increased cable penetration has impacted—and will no doubt continue to impact—the structure of both audience shares and revenues within the telecommunication industry. A recent study (Krugman and Rust, 1987) investigated cable penetration, network shares, network revenues and cable revenues per cable household. Table 5.3 shows current 1985 figures and 1990 and year 2000 projections. Network share of audience and revenues will decline, yet still account for the vast majority of advertising revenues. However, this projection is based on advertisers feeling the same way about the ability of networks to deliver a "critical mass" in terms of audience shares. If the projected 54.6 network audience share falls below a threshold of confidence in the ability of networks to deliver audiences, then network revenues could drop dramatically. Advertising revenues per cable household are expected to almost double from 1985 to the year 2000. This certainly confirms the idea of a very active cable industry which competes for advertising revenues.

While it is difficult to know what the reach threshold is for national advertisers, it is very likely that the tendency to stay with the networks will not hold as firmly in the future as in the past. Obviously, there will be a reach threshold, below which networks will not be able to hold their advertising revenues to a point disproportionately higher than their actual ratings.

The cable industry is aggressive and becoming much more savvy in terms of marketing both their programming and their basic subscriptions. Advertising revenues over cable are now $1.3 billion. We used to think of local cable operators as not terribly sophisticated in understanding their local subscribers. Basically, they were viewed as local monopolies. A look at the hiring of local station managers reveals that the times have changed.

Firms are now hiring MBAs to run local franchises. This step, I think, is the forerunner of a very big push for local cable advertising revenues. The impact will be competition for radio as well as local spot television.

Frederick Williams observed in 1987 that the future of new communication technologies is in advertising revenues:

> A key question about new communication technologies, especially those that might compete with traditional media, is the degree to which they can capture advertising revenues. Although cable began with, and continues to be mostly a subscription fee medium, many analysts see its eventual major growth in the form of advertising revenues. (Williams, 1987:155–56)

Research studies clearly indicate that cable viewing is becoming more specialized and that specific segments are forming. Additionally, television technologies have created a scenario in which the decision to watch and the actual watching are potentially more active. This segmented viewing may not replace much of the current viewing, but it will compliment viewing. Advertisers need to recast much of their predispositions about the viewer-television relationship. This does not mean a more hostile environment to distribute the message. It certainly does mean a different environment and one where programming and advertising have more in common. Additionally, we should be wary of always trying to separate our understanding of commercial viewing from our understanding of program viewing. Commercial viewing needs to be investigated within the total framework of program viewing.

At the moment we make fairly clear distinctions between commercially sponsored television programming and pay-premium/VCR rental entertainment. This distinction will be increasingly blurred. A combination of commercial/pay services are in the future To a degree, they are here now in two different fashions; tiered cable and PPV sports packages that have some advertising.

In 1978 and 1982, it was argued that pay cable advertising was on the horizon (Krugman and Barban, 1978; 1982). Bogart (1986) also noted the possibility of pay cable advertising. Initial indications are that consumers are not against the notion of advertising on pay cable channels. Advertising revenues can help stabilize or lower the costs of pay programming. Most of the individuals in these audiences are upscale and highly desirable to advertisers. Therefore, advertisers will go to great lengths to access them. Viewers will become increasingly accustomed to paying for television. Paying for specialized programming and watching commercials will not continue to be seen as disparate. To this same extent we can expect advertising on more and more VCR rentals.

Younger audiences, growing up in a more select, controllable, and at times more active viewing environment, have different expectations. The advertising formats of today are in need of a rethinking. What advertising and media planners must increasingly understand is the quality of viewing for these specialized audiences, rather than just the quantity of those viewers.

Finally, two additional items arise. One is the polarization of media use based on the combination of viewing technologies and services. The noncable home with a VCR is much different than the noncable home without one. We need to have an understanding of how markets differ based on multiple ownership patterns.

6

Collecting Ratings Data for Cable Channels

Seymour Sudman

Introduction

The purpose of this chapter is to examine alternative methods for collecting rating data for cable channels. If one wishes to make this task more difficult, one could specify obtaining information in *local* markets, as was the purpose of the Cable Audience Methodology Study (CAMS) conducted for the Cablevision Advertising Bureau and the National Cable Television Association by the A. C. Nielsen Company (Nielsen, 1983).

The task would not be difficult if there were no financial constraints. Indeed the methods used now could simply be adopted with much larger samples. Unfortunately, finances are the heart of the problem. The users of cable measurement services would probably be unwilling to spend as much as current users of the national ratings services spend, let alone spend much, much more.

The reasons for this have nothing to do with the sophistication of cable television researchers, or with their desire for high-quality research. The reasons are purely economic. Although cable researchers would like to have research that matches or exceeds the quality of current research, they just do not have the market shares and revenue to afford it. Of course, the situation could change if cable market shares rose sharply, or if new technologies are developed; and some discussion of this is given in the next part. In the rest of this chapter it is assumed that current conditions will continue.

A useful analogy can be made with efforts to improve radio measurement services. Several years ago, two of the largest market research suppliers proposed new and improved methods for measuring radio audiences. Despite the clear need for such improvements, user demand was insufficient to get them off the ground because the costs were too great.

It is always the role of the research supplier to offer the best methods that exist within constraints of likely costs. This is what I shall attempt to do, recognizing that these procedures would not be the best ones if more money was available.

The Use of Meters

The CAMS study that I referred to did not consider meters as one of the possible alternatives, probably because of cost, but also because people meters were not yet perfected and tested when the study was conducted. I would agree that the cost of meters at this time precludes their use everywhere, but it is possible that there will be technological or other developments that may make meters a feasible alternative for measuring cable viewing.

The basic development necessary is the reduction of the cost of the meters. This is not at all impossible given the drop in costs that we have already seen. Another highly desirable development would be the development of a meter which either required no wiring or was so simple to wire that it could be done without sending a technician to the home. This would eliminate the expensive personal visit since households could then be recruited by telephone or possibly even by mail. None of this will happen tomorrow, but it does not seem unduly optimistic to anticipate that this may happen in the next decade. Even today, it may be possible to use meters in some of the largest cities by combining results from competing firms in those sites and possibly by supplementing with additional meter households. While the results in the largest cities cannot be used to directly generalize elsewhere, they can be used as a measure of the deficiencies in the collection procedures used in smaller areas. It is also possible that as network shares of total audience shrink, the current measuring services will need to increase their sample size to maintain current accuracy levels. This would, of course, simultaneously improve the accuracy of measures of cable viewing.

There are two major drawbacks to the use of meters, even if the technology reduces their cost. The first, and most obvious, is that even with major cost reductions meters will always be more expensive than other methods to buy, service, and mail. While meters are less costly to process, the net advantage will still be with the current procedures. For local cable measurement in smaller markets, a meter service with greatly reduced costs might still be too expensive.

It must also be recognized that although people meters are the standard by which alternative procedures are evaluated, people meters are also subject to possible survey biases and errors of measurement. The first bias

Table 6.1
Percentage of Households using Television among Nielsen Panel for Cooperation and Total Sample

Time	Nielsen Panel Cooperators	Total Sample
Total all hours	45.3	43.9
Total daytime hours	29.2	27.8
10-11 a.m.	23.8	22.1
2-3 p.m.	25.1	24.7
5-6 p.m.	38.6	36.7
Total Nighttime hours	61.4	60.1
7-8 p.m.	57.3	56.8
8-9 p.m.	63.8	61.9
9-10 p.m.	63.3	61.4
Sample Size	18,843	18,228

source is caused by the fact that only about half the households recruited to participate in meter panels agree to do so. (I have not seen comparable data for people meters, but it is likely that similar results would be observed.) It has generally been found that there are no significant biases in the channels or types of programs watched when panel households are compared to those who will not cooperate. The bias that is observed is that meter panel households are slightly more likely to watch television than are households who refuse to cooperate (see table 6.1) (Cordell and Rahmel, 1962). Since the bias is only about 1.5 percentage points it has generally been ignored by the industry.

The use of people meters intuitively would appear to be more accurate than other methods that require the household to keep written records. Nevertheless, there will be some individuals who will sometimes forget to press their buttons when they enter or leave the viewing area. The reports to date would suggest that the net effects of such errors will be small and will be ignored by the industry.

It has not been clear whether there will be a people meter for every television set in the household, or only a single people meter per household.

This will be an important issue for the cable industry, since there is the possibility that viewing of cable stations will be higher in multiple-set households. This is not really a flaw of people meters unless their construction makes it impossible to have multiple meters in the same household because of interference problems.

I also recognize that my suggestion that meter services be combined with diary methods would cause difficulties among users of these services. While statisticians have no difficulty in designing and using complex estimates from multiple sources, most users of cable ratings will prefer procedures that are straightforward and easy to understand and explain. There is also a strong desire for standardized services in each local market so that users do not need to be concerned with differences caused by alternative data collection methods.

To summarize, there are obvious methodological advantages of the use of meters and people meters for measuring cable viewing, but the costs make this unrealistic at this time. Even with likely technological developments that will reduce meter costs substantially, it is unlikely that meters will become cheap enough to replace the current method used in local markets to measure cable viewing.

Household Diaries

The standard procedure in areas where meters have been too expensive to use has been to use written diaries. It would seem logical to use these for measurement of cable services as well. The CAMS study shows a distressing finding, however, for those who wish to measure cable accurately. Compared with telephone coincidental data collection, reports of the use of cable in the household and by persons within the household are understated by about 50%. (See tables 6.2 and 6.3, which reproduce tables 11 and 19 of the CAMS report.) Table 6.2 presents data for persons age 12 and over while table 6.3 presents data for households. The results are very similar. This is for the standard seven-day diary; much better results for cable, but worse for other stations, are reported for half-hour personal diaries that we will discuss later.

What is going on? Why do these differ? First, it should be noted that these are based on ratings of 5% or less and shares of 25% or less. Some of this could be sampling variability. If there are real methods differences, however, they could be the results of deficiencies in the telephone coincidental or diary methods or a combination of both.

People responding on the telephone could simply mistake a network situation for a cable station, or they might be overreporting a cable station

Table 6.2
Ratings Analysis of Persons 12+ Monday-Friday 9:00 A.M. - 11:00 P.M.

Category	Coinci-dental	7-day unaided recall	1-day aided recall	Personal diaries half-hour diary	Household diaries NSI diary
Broadcast networks					
Rating	10.1	12.0	12.4	19.7	9.9
Share	52.7	63.6	61.3	63.5	65.1
Broadcast independents					
Rating	3.0	3.1	2.6	5.2	2.6
Share	15.8	16.2	13.0	16.8	16.5
Basic cable					
Rating	3.1	1.8	2.5	4.4	1.4
Share	16.4	9.3	12.2	14.3	9.3
Pay cable					
Rating	2.0	1.1	1.7	2.1	1.0
Share	10.3	5.9	8.3	6.7	6.9
PUTS	19.1	18.9	20.2	31.0	15.4

because that is a more socially desirable answer than the station they are actually listening to. Similar patterns have been observed with other media, such as public broadcasting. Relatively few people would need to err to cause the patterns seen in this report.

On the other hand, the diary panel could also be in error. Three major reasons suggest themselves—memory error, conditioning, or sample bias.

Memory Error

If the diary keeper always kept the diary at hand and made entries as the event occurred (the program was being watched) there would be perfect reporting. Probably some diary keepers do follow such an immediate entry system. Others, however, forget or choose not to make immediate entries,

Table 6.3
Household Rating and Share Estimates Monday-Friday 9:00 A.M. - 11:00 P.M.

Category of Programming	Coincidental	Standard NSI
Broadcast Networks		
Ratings	17.6	21.5
Share	53.1	66.0
Broadcast Independents		
Ratings	6.2	6.0
Share	18.7	18.5
Basic Cable		
Ratings	5.4	3.4
Share	16.3	10.4
Pay Cable		
Ratings	3.0	1.9
Share	9.1	5.8
Homes Using Television (HUT)	33.2	32.6

but to construct their household's viewing behavior at the end of each day or sometimes at the end of the seven days. Thus memory error becomes a real possibility.

We shall discuss two kinds of memory error: simple omissions and incorrect recall. Simple omissions are caused by forgetting that an event occurred, which is related to several factors. The first is simply time. If a diary keeper waits until the end of seven days, it will be far more difficult to remember specific events than if the diary keeper records at the end of each day or every few hours.

A second factor is that it is far easier to remember things that have happened to us than to others in the household. If all members of the household are doing the same thing, then this is not a problem; but if some members are watching television while others are not, or if some are watching a different program than the diary keeper, this will be more difficult to remember. The task is made still more difficult if other household members are not visible and do not report their television viewing behavior to the person keeping the diary. This is a major advantage of personal diaries that are discussed in the next section.

When the memory task of remembering all the details of specific events becomes too difficult, people use estimation procedures based on typical behavior. Cognitive psychologists have studied the mechanisms that are used. See, for example, Strack and Martin in Hippler et al. (1987). In addition to memory, some diary keepers may assume that they should report their typical behavior although they are watching something else at that time period during the diary week. If cable viewing is unusual and sporadic, it is likely that it will be underestimated.

The diary used in the CAMS methodology did not list the possible stations for the respondent. If the stations had been listed, the memory task might have been made easier for the diary keeper, and more cable stations might have been reported.

Conditioning

For diary keepers, conditioning refers to changes in behavior as a result of keeping the diary. It is certainly possible that keeping a diary reminds the diary keeper about the behavior, and may thus increase the behavior. This has been noted in the initial period for several different types of diary data collection:

1. In the 1972–73 Consumer Expenditure Survey conducted by the U.S. Bureau of the Census with 20,000 households, a diary record of food and beverage expenditures was kept for a two-week period. Expenditures in the first week were 10% higher than those in the second week. There was no evidence that this was due to any special product classes. The same results were seen for all of the food and beverage categories.
2. In a 1969 pilot study conducted by the Survey Research Laboratory that preceded the 1972–73 Consumer Expenditure Survey, expenditures in the first week were 8% higher than in the second week.
3. In a 1973–74 study conducted by the Survey Research Laboratory on the use of diaries in reporting medical events, a sample of Illinois and Wisconsin residents kept records for three months. The total number of events recorded was 14% higher in month one than in months two and three (Sudman and Ferber, 1979: 86).

There is no comparable evidence of such an effect on television viewing, because the standard period used for diary keepers is one week. Nevertheless, one might well expect the same kind of effect, although its magnitude would be impossible to estimate. The effect would be greatest if the diary keepers reported only their own behavior, and would be diminished if household viewing was reported since the determination of what to watch would not be entirely that of the diary keeper. PBlBlP

Sample Bias

It is well-known that asking households or individuals to keep written diaries substantially increases the noncooperation level over that found on a single interview. The current diary methods that recruit households by mail and request them to keep a diary for a seven-day period obtain cooperation rates of around 50%. Interestingly, this is about the same rate of cooperation obtained in the long run in meter households that are recruited in person. That is, the sample biases of meters and diaries are of the same magnitude.

The key question, of course, is what the effects are of the sample biases on the data. Since reading and writing are required for diary keeping, one would expect that education would be a factor, as it is for most mail surveys. This is the case for households where the head has eight grades of school or less, but the percentage in this group continues to drop.

Another bias found in all diary samples is a shortage of small households consisting of one or two members, but especially of single-member households. While diary keeping is easiest for such individuals, they are least likely to be found at home. The obvious corollary is that diary samples have too many households with children and too few without.

For other demographic variables, no differences are seen between those willing and unwilling to keep diary records. The key question is whether there are behavioral differences. The answer is that those to whom the behavior is most salient are most willing to keep diary records of that behavior.

For purchase panels, there is weak evidence to suggest that those willing to keep diaries are more concerned about shopping than are those unwilling to keep diaries. Among diary keepers, 41% considered themselves to be more price conscious than average, compared to 33% of those unwilling to keep diaries (Sudman and Ferber, 1979: 34).

The same pattern has been observed for television viewer panels. That is, participants in viewer panels are more interested in television and watch slightly more than do those who are unwilling to participate in viewer panels, as was seen in table 6.1. While this is a study of the meter panels, results for the diary panels are similar.

There is no evidence that sample biases cause any distortion in the distribution of channels watched by those who are watching television. This is also the case in purchase panels where there is little evidence of distortion in brands purchased.

To summarize, sample biases do exist in diary panels of viewing or any other behavior. For television viewing, the effect of the biases is to slightly increase total viewing while not affecting the distribution of programs and channels watched. Since the sample biases exist for meters, this is not a defect that is unique to diary methods.

Personal Diaries

The major problem with household diaries is that they may miss viewing by others in the household, particularly teenagers. The personal diary solves this problem, as may be seen in tables 6.2 and 6.3. However, CAMS data suggest that this method substantially overreports all forms of viewing. Again there are two alternatives. It may be that the diary is correct, and the telephone coincidental method omits viewers who are watching second sets and do not answer the telephone. The other possibility, as discussed in the previous section, is that individual television viewing is being conditioned by the diary keeping and that unusual behavior is occurring as the result of an individual keeping the diary.

There are two other format differences that may account for some of the differences between the personal and household diaries. In the personal diaries, the time periods used were half-hour rather than quarter-hour segments. Also in the personal diaries, the diary keepers were given a list of the local channels to aid their memory, while this was not done in the standard household diary.

I know of no evidence that would suggest that there should be major changes in level of viewing because of the difference between quarter- and half-hour segments, although this is a possibility. The use of a list of all local channels may well improve the recall of cable stations, although again there is no supporting evidence. What is clear is that the use of personal diaries would be expected to improve reporting based on our earlier discussion of reporting errors and, indeed, it does.

The fact that conditioning may be causing increased viewing by persons who keep the personal diary does not necessarily mean that this method cannot be used. As suggested earlier, using a two-week instead of one-week period, as is done for consumer expenditures, would probably provide more valid information. From my perspective, the use of personal diaries is sufficiently promising to warrant additional testing.

All else equal, cost considerations favor household over individual diaries. The advantages of personal diaries for measuring cable watching may be strong enough to justify their added cost. A compromise solution is the use of household diaries with sufficient supplementation of personal diaries to make it possible to measure special channels such as MTV.

In summary, the point I wish to stress is that it would be premature to eliminate diaries from consideration as a method for measuring cable usage in local markets. There may be methods for improving the diary such as adding checkboxes at the top to remind the diary keeper to include cable stations, or additional instructions in the material that is sent to households. I understand that diaries now being used in local areas do list the stations in that area, so that respondents have an easier memory task.

There is also a sense of déjà vu in the comparisons between coincidental telephone and diary procedures. Several decades ago such comparisons were made in early issues of the Journal of Advertising Research and by CONTAM (The Committee on Nationwide Television Audience Measurement). See for example Ehrenberg (1962), Hooper (1966), and CONTAM (1971). Almost every study found some differences between methods. These differences were sometimes attributed to faults in the diary/meter procedures and sometimes to faults in the telephone coincidental methods. Thus, for example, the CONTAM findings were as follows:

1. Home rating levels were caused to be understated by the assumptions usually made in conventional coincidental rating surveys.
2. The CONTAM and simulated conventional methods produced virtually identical Viewers Per Tuning Household estimates. Audience composition was essentially the same for the two methods.
3. The two telephone coincidental methods produced virtually the same results for program share of audience.
4. Nielsen Viewers Per Tuning Household were slightly below the levels attained from the carefully conducted coincidental. Young adults, teenagers, and children in particular tended to be lower in the diary estimates.
5. Share of audience estimates produced by CONTAM were very close to those made by Nielsen.
6. In general, the findings for daytime confirmed in every instance the findings for prime time.

Eventually the cost advantages of diaries overcame methodological concerns. The same thing may well happen again.

Telephone One-Day Recall

Both telephone methods tested involved the use of one-day recall. The difference between the two procedures was that in one case respondents did this for only a single day, while in the other procedure they were called on seven consecutive days. Not surprisingly, the cooperation rate was much higher for one than for seven days. The seven-day cooperation rate was comparable to that obtained with diaries.

The differences in sample cooperation do not appear to have any general effect on the results, however. To my eyes, the differences between the one and seven-day recall groups are not consistent and probably reflect sampling errors.

There are no clear-cut advantages of recall versus diaries in the quality of results, but there are substantial cost differences. Daily telephone interviews are more expensive than weekly diaries whether a respondent is called once or seven times. Thus, as with the current television ratings services, diary methods dominate recall procedures for continuous measurement of viewing.

Sampling Issues

There are no major new sampling issues that arise from a need to measure cable ratings. The sampling issues are similar to those raised in obtaining radio and magazine ratings. That is, it is necessary to measure small percentages with reasonable accuracy. Unlike magazines, but similar to radio, it is also necessary to measure these small percentages in many different geographic areas separately.

The obvious solution is to obtain information from very large samples. This, of course, becomes very expensive, especially if measurement is continuous or even frequent. One obvious solution is to reduce the frequency of measurement. Annual—or even less frequent—measurements may become affordable.

The wide variability in the availability of cable services by community, and advertiser strategies that require local information, lead to multi-stage designs with much larger clusters than are used even in current local television measurement. For ratings, no alternatives are likely.

It does seem possible that one would like to measure attitudes toward a cable station and uses of its services. For this purpose, one needs a sample of users of that station, perhaps split by intensity of use. Obviously, the users of pay supplementary services such as HBO and The Disney Channel can be identified from the billing records of local cable operators. Assuming reasonable cooperation from these operators, list samples would be easy to generate.

On a broader scale, it would be possible to send mail surveys to cable subscribers to obtain information on general usage of cable television and to screen for users of specific cable stations. One would expect reasonably good response if the survey is well executed, similar to the careful studies of readers that have been conduced by the print media.

The use of cable subscriber lists would also make it possible to identify households who have recently added, cancelled, or changed their cable services so they could be questioned about the reasons for the changes. Again, all of this assumes that there are sufficient resources and interest to conduct such research. At the final stage of sampling, that is, within the household, the respondent(s) should be the viewers of the specific cable channel studied.

Earlier in this paper we discussed panel methods for collecting ratings data for cable channels. There is a need, however, to understand detailed patterns of viewing of cable channels that probably will not be met by the more general ratings services. For this purpose, it would be appropriate to identify viewers of specific channels and to recruit these viewers into a panel, using either meters or diaries.

These panels could consist of either households or individuals, depending on the needs of the research. For measuring channel viewing of teenagers or children, it would be critical that all household sets be metered or that personal diaries be kept by individual household members. One difference from the current procedures that obtain one week's viewing is that it will probably take a longer period—a month or possibly even longer—to get accurate viewing patterns for some cable stations.

Summary

In this chapter, we have discussed alternative methods for collecting cable station ratings data. There is really very little that is new in this discussion. Essentially the problems faced by cable researchers are the same as those faced by researchers attempting to measure radio listening and magazine reading. The audience is very fragmented; therefore, sampling variances for any collection method are large, unless very large and costly samples are selected.

Because of this cost problem it may not be economically feasible to obtain continuous measures of cable viewing. Rather, as with radio and magazines, researchers may have to be satisfied with periodic, perhaps annual, studies. Field work for these studies could be conducted continuously, but the data reported only when the sample becomes large enough.

At this point in time, the use of meters for a sample large enough to measure cable stations does not seem to be economically viable. What would be necessary to even consider meters would be the continuing development of inexpensive meters that require no special installation. Even in this case, however, the use of meters for large local samples may still be too expensive relative to the diary methods now used.

These diary methods will continue to receive wide use for the measurement of cable viewing, not because they are perfect, but because they provide an economically feasible data collection method. Even with potential sample biases and possible reporting errors, diaries dominate telephone recall methods because of their lower costs.

Personal diaries are more accurate than household diaries because individuals know more about their own behavior and are better able to remember it. The use of a two-week period may help reduce some of the high levels of viewing caused by keeping the diary. Personal diaries are especially important for measuring viewing of children and teenagers of channels such as MTV, on second or third sets.

In the final part of this chapter, we discuss alternatives to simple ratings measures that would be similar to the studies ofsubscribers that are conducted by magazines. These studies would first locate viewers of specific cable channels using subscriber lists and mail screening. These viewers would then be requested to report on attitudes toward and uses of the specific channel. In some cases, these viewers might be recruited to a panel to obtain detailed viewing information over time. Such studies provide information that cannot be obtained from simply looking at ratings. As with large magazine subscriber studies, however, the cost and difficulty of such special studies would limit their frequency.

7

When Does Greater Program Impact Lead to Greater Advertising Impact?

Rajeev Batra

Introduction

Previous research has shown that, on the average, only about 50% of the people in the room with a TV set on will watch an ad (which means that most advertisers' reach estimates are off by a factor of two). Such research also suggests major differences in such percentages across dayparts: the range extends from 43% to 58%, which implies tremendous advertising leverage if dayparts (and, by extension, programs) are selected to maximize such percentages. In short, programs *do* appear to differ in the degree to which program viewing carries over to the viewing of commercials embedded in them.

Cable networks have long claimed that their smaller, specialized audiences find cable programs more "involving," and that advertising works better in such narrowcasting environments, allegedly justifying higher CPMs. (I have before me an ad in *Advertising Age* in which one cable network claims that they bring people "high involvement TV," instead of "ho-hum TV, the kind you half watch while your eyes glaze over and your soda spills on the couch.") Is more "involving" programming really better for advertising commercials? Can cable advertising really claim that ads work better in its more compatible editorial environment? And, if yes, what kinds of ads are most effective in what kinds of program environments?

I develop in this chapter a theoretical framework in which such issues may be examined empirically, in the belief that the claim of cable networks to greater advertising effectiveness can only be supported when such em-

pirical studies are conducted. It is hoped that the ideas presented here will
provide the impetus to such empirical research.

It is not as if there are no prior data to support the contention of the
cable networks. Hoffman (1984) reports, for example, that "high impact"
programs are, in fact, watched with fewer people indulging in competing
activities and walking out of the room; which means that such high impact
programs are watched with greater attention and longer look lengths. Thus,
there do seem to be some data supporting the hypothesis that it is better
to advertise in high impact programs, at least if you are the first commercial
in a string.

However, not all the previous research on this topic is so unequivocal.
Research on the relationship between the level of audience involvement
in television programming (sometimes called program impact or interest)
and the effectiveness of advertising placed in or around these programs is
at least 30 years old. These studies have shown that such program/ad
interactions exist and deserve both managerial and theoretical attention,
because their effects have important implications for media placement
methods (e.g., Siebert [1978] on Burke DAR consequences of program
environment), and for our understanding of how television advertising
works (both Stiener [1966] and Soldow and Principe [1981] use the "attitude to the interrrupting ad" as a mediating variable for ad effectiveness
in general).

Unfortunately, however, such research has shown that high involvement
in program content affects commercial effectiveness both positively
(through hypothesized "carryover" effects) and negatively (through hypothesized resentment against ads that "interrupt" involving programming), depending on the study. What is needed now is a systematic
theoretical framework that resolves these conflicting results.

Recent research into the processing of advertising messages suggests that
the inconsistent results of earlier studies are not only understandable but
also should have been expected, because the effect of program involvement
on commercial effectiveness should depend on a whole host of other factors—just as the ways in which advertising works in general depend on
many factors (see, for example, Petty and Cacioppo [1979]). In the rest of
this chapter, I begin the attempt to develop a theoretical framework for
the experimental investigation of these "contingent effects" of program
environment on advertising effectiveness.

Previous Research: Program "Involvement" and Ad Effectiveness

Since our concern is with the relationship between program involvement
levels and ad effectiveness, we first must make clear what we mean by the
terms "program involvement" and "ad effectiveness."

A review of previous definitions of "program involvement" used in the literature may be found in Television Audience Assessment (1984a): most researchers include both the "personal relevance" of the program and its "entertainment value." Television Audience Assessment itself includes, in "program involvement," both a program's (entertainment) "appeal" and its (intellectual and emotional) "impact." Recent research by Hoffman (1984) suggests that the latter "impact" should not be treated as unidimensional, but that its "emotional" and "cognitive" elements should be treated separately. For the moment, it should be noted merely that the research discussed below combines the entertainment, arousal, emotional depth, and intellectual and cognitive elements of a program in its degree of "involvement."

Nor is there much agreement on the one best measure of ad effectiveness: studies measure effects on ad recall, attitude towards the ad, attitude to the brand, and brand purchase intentions, as alternative measures of ad "effectiveness." As will become apparent, program effects often vary across these different measures.

Most studies using such definitions in investigating the effects of TV program involvement levels on advertising commercial effectiveness have found some effects (Barry [1962] is probably the only exception). They have differed, however, in the direction of the effects found: positive or negative.

One stream of studies has hypothesized, and sometimes found, a positive relationship between the level of program involvement and advertising commercial effectiveness. These studies argue for this effect in two related ways.

First, it is argued that programming that is more involving creates higher levels of intrinsic attention which carry over to the advertising commercials shown during those programs, as long as those commercials are themselves interesting (Krugman, 1983; Twyman, 1974; Clancy and Kweskin, 1971; Schwerin, 1960; Barclay, Doub, and McMurtrey 1965; Home Testing Institute, 1963; Smith, 1956).

Other studies add that more interesting programming causes fewer viewers to leave the room during the program or during commercial breaks, and that these viewers tend to engage in fewer distracting behaviors (such as reading or talking) while the programs and ads are on (Television Audience Assessment, 1983; Hoffman, 1984). The high frequency of such behaviors, and their impact on commercial effectiveness, has been documented repeatedly. A reduction in such distracting behaviors implies greater attention to the ads, leading to higher recall and/or persuasion (Nuttall, 1962; Smith, 1956; Eyes on Television, 1980; Twyman, 1974; Television Audience Assessment, 1984a and 1984b).

A second set of studies, however, argues that higher audience involvement in the television program will actually hurt advertising effectiveness.

Such studies argue that viewers who are more involved in such programs resent the commercials that come on and interrupt those programs, and thus dislike those commercials and, by implication, those brands advertised (Steiner, 1966; Kennedy, 1971; Schwerin, 1958; Soldow and Principe, 1981).

Both viewpoints are plausible, and both sets of results have been found (though the preponderance of evidence supports the first, "positive transfer" viewpoint). Clearly, some of this variance in results is attributable to differences in methodologies used in the different studies, and even to differences in the way "program involvement" is operationalized in any particular study.

However, not only do empirical results differ across studies, they often differ within studies as well: the direction of the relationship varies for the product category used in the ad (Yuspeh, 1979; Kennedy, 1971; Soldow and Principe, 1981), ad execution style (Kennedy, 1971), ad position within program (Soldow and Principe, 1981; Barclay et al., 1965), and effectiveness measure used (e.g., aided versus unaided recall: Kennedy, 1971; Murphy et al. 1979).

Clearly it seems likely, given such interactions, that the effect of program involvement level on advertising effectiveness is moderated by a variety of other factors. What is needed is a systematic delineation of what these factors are and how they interact, rather than post-hoc attempts to explain away inconsistencies from a monolithic "one type of transfer" view of how program involvement affects ad effectiveness. Below, an attempt is made to develop such a theoretical scheme, generating testable hypotheses.

Suggested Theoretical Framework

The starting point, based on the preponderance of research results just discussed, is that the basic direction of the relationship between program involvement and advertising effectiveness is positive. However, it is suggested that this relationship is moderated by, and is contingent on, a number of other factors.

In particular, I believe the relationship depends on (1) the viewer's motivational involvement with the specific product category featured in the ad, called "product category involvement," and (2) the execution style of the ad, whether affective or rational. Such interactions have appeared in much previous research, reviewed earlier. These interactions are of special interest because they appear to be crucial determinants of the "routes" through which advertising works, as specified in recent research on advertising information processing (e.g., Petty and Cacioppo, 1979).

Just as this recent research shows the route of advertising effectiveness to depend on the interaction of the execution style of the ad and the level of (cognitive) product category involvement, so also do I believe that the type of ad execution and the *type* of program involvement (in addition to its level) are important variables in determining program/ad carryovers.

To do this, we must show that program involvement is not unidimensional. Indeed, based on the work of Hoffman (1984), it does appear that program involvement (or program impact, as Hoffman calls it), is of two distinct kinds: cognitive and affective. A program that "touches your feelings" is of a different type than one which "you learn something from." Current conceptions and operationalizations of program impact combine these two different kinds: Television Audience Assessment Inc., for example, combines both the intellectual and emotional stimulation from a TV program into one composite "Program Impact" index (1984b). Hoffman's analysis, on the other hand, suggests that programs that are high on one kind of impact may not be high on another. Thus I believe these two kinds of impact should be modeled separately; the appropriateness of the kind of program impact, to the kind of commercial in question, may moderate the relationship observed.

Having argued for two types of ad executions (affective and rational, as theoretical extremes) and for two types of program impact, the crucial element in the theoretical scheme becomes the consistency between the two. It is suggested that, for the program impact-to-ad effectiveness link to exist, the *kind* of program impact (i.e., cognitive versus affective) must match the *kind* of creative execution style used in the commercial (rational versus emotional). That is, high program impact will carry over to ad execution effectiveness only if both the program and ad are similar in emotional/rational orientation.

This expectation is based on various streams of literature. There is, first, the literature on media environmental effects, which argues for such "congruence effects" (Stanton and Lowenhar, 1977; Horn and McEwen, 1977; Crane, 1964; Axelrod, 1963). Next, research in cognitive social psychology supports such reasoning (Isen et al., 1982; Bower and Cohen, 1982; see also Rapaport, 1961). Such research suggests that viewers watching an impactful program of high *affective* intensity may be differentially likely to notice, process, and favorably judge stimuli (ads) that rely on emotional appeals for their effectiveness.

Such viewers are unlikely to process deeply (i.e., in attribute terms) those ads relying instead on attribute superiority arguments; they will generate fewer cognitive responses, making the message less impactful (cf. Petty and Cacioppo, 1979). Conversely, viewers placed in a rational, thoughtful frame of mind through a high impact program of the cognitive variety will process rational ads in the attribute-intensive way that such ads are meant to be processed, increasing their effectiveness; but these viewers are likely to be resistant to emotional appeals.

However, it is expected that this differential transfer from program to ad effectiveness will occur only under certain levels of involvement with the product category featured in the ad. When such motivational involvement is high, the viewer is expected to deeply process the brand attribute arguments presented in the ad regardless of the program environment. The expected interactions are not therefore expected to occur in such situations. In low motivational involvement (with the product category), however, the expected interactions are expected to occur, and such "type congruence" is expected to be important (cf. Isen et al., 1982). Such product class interactions were observed earlier by Yuspeh (1979), Soldow and Principe (1981), and Kennedy (1971), among others, though any interpretation of them in terms of "product class involvement" is obviously post-hoc in nature.

Finally, it is expected that these interactions will occur only for some measures of ad effectiveness and not for others, but—given inadequate theory—they will not be formalized as hypotheses here. The other theoretical speculations presented above are now formally expressed as testable hypotheses:

H1. If program impact is high, type of impact being cognitive (rational), then attribute-intensive (rational) ads will perform better than affective ads for low product category involvement products.

H2. If program impact is high, type of impact being affective (emotional), then emotional ads will perform better than rational ads for low product category involvement products.

H3. If program impact is low, there will be no difference in ad effectiveness as a function of ad execution style/type of program impact, for both high (H3a) and low (H3b) involvement product categories.

H4. If product category involvement is low, there will be no difference in ad effectiveness as a function of ad execution style/type of program impact, for both high (H4a) and low (H4b) program impact levels.

Conclusion

Given some testable hypotheses (and there could clearly be others), what is needed now is the step beyond research showing that TV programs differ in their "impact" levels. We now need research showing conclusively and unequivocally how such program impact translates into advertising effectiveness, under a variety of theoretically meaningful circumstances. Such research could be of great value not only to managers developing media plans but also to academics interested in increasing our understanding of how advertising works.

8

Discussion on Chapters 5 and 6

David H. Harkness, Jack Hill, and Jonathan B. Sims

A. Comments on Chapter 6 by David Harkness
(A. C. Nielsen Company)

I agree with most of the comments made by Dr. Sudman. The diary is not a perfect measurement tool; but then again, no method is. All measurements have inherent limitations. What seems to have no limitations is the viewing environment, which is becoming more and more difficult to measure every day, even electronically. There's always something new. The latest challenge is digital TVs with multiple tuners and rabbits. Rabbits are multiplying like crazy.

I would like to address a few comments to points Dr. Sudman in chapter 6:

First, CAMS was a study of the diary at one point in time, five years ago. Most of the cable program services were fairly new. Viewers are more familiar with cable now and may, therefore, be more able to correctly indicate their cable viewing. We should keep this in mind and exercise some caution in interpreting findings from a 5-year-old study.

Second, the NSI diary that was tested in the CAMS study has been substantially modified since 1982. One of the modifications includes a roster of channels carried by the respondents' cable system, which is included in the materials mailed to the household. It was mentioned that differences observed between the household and personal diary were not likely to be caused by differences in format. I'm not sure I agree with this, as the personal diary included a roster of the cable channels programmed. The personal diary employed a half-hour format instead of a quarter-hour format as used in the NSI diary. Both of these factors probably contributed to the reporting of higher viewing levels.

Third, the NSI diary can be used effectively for cable measurement applications in ways that avoid many diary limitations. One example is that the diary can be used to measure the number of viewers per viewing household (VPVH) for cable network programming. The number of viewers per viewing household of a demographic break can be multiplied by the number of households tuned to that program as determined by our national sample of metered households. In this way, demographic viewing projections are made.

We completed a national telephone coincidental survey sponsored by the cable networks in which 310,000 households were called. Our conclusion was that on a VPVH basis, the diary could be used to measure most cable networks. There were some exceptions, especially in the area of teen measurement.

The diary can be used to establish relative differences in cable network viewing levels from one cable system or interconnect to another. Nielsen currently offers a local cable audience measurement service we call CAP or Cable Audience Profile. CAP is a local cable audience measurement method which compares the cable network viewing from a system or interconnect to a national average of viewing to the same cable networks. The result of this comparison is expressed in the form of an index.

Fourth, I have several comments on the issue of a low-cost, easy-to-install meter for cable measurement. I assume that this meter would be used for local market cable measurement, since cable has been measured on a national basis by our national metered sample for about seven years now. By this time next year we will have a 5,000 household people meter panel in place which will be more than adequate for national cable measurement needs.

On a local system basis, I do not perceive the barrier to electronic measurement, or an easy-to-install low-cost meter, to be a technology issue, but a marketplace issue. To evaluate the potential for a product, one must start with an assessment of the market need for that product. What is the marketplace need for local cable system audience research, and what value does the customer place on the research (value being the ratio of benefits divided by cost in the eyes of the customer)?

Although local cable ad sales is a substantial growth area for cable operators, coverage areas are limited and, therefore, ad sales revenue potential (as compared to a local market broadcaster) is not as large. Therefore, the value of viewing reports are less. We have set a goal for ourselves of being able to supply an affordable audience measurement service for cable operators. Our CAP reports are very cost efficient. Metered measurement is considerably more expensive.

Breakthrough technology—that is, the so-called mailable meter—is not likely to meet the current marketplace need, since one could eliminate the metering cost entirely from the cost equalization. Consider only the permissioning expense, the incentives required, the data processing and data publication expense, and I believe you will still find very few cable operators interested in electronic measurement—not when viewed against the alternatives, which may cost only a few thousand dollars. The limiting factor is not technology, but marketplace need.

Comments on Chapter 6 by Jack Hill (CableTelevision Advertising Bureau)

After reading Dr. Sudman's remarks about the CAMS study, you may well wonder why the cable industry ever bothered. Let me begin by acknowledging that we got off to a bad start by insisting that cable was a new and different medium and therefore not amenable to existing measure of audience.

As a member of the ad hoc group of researchers who developed the design of the CAMS study in the early eighties, I shared their belief that cable's main strength as an advertising medium would be local, and that the first priority was to find a local measurement capable of measuring viewing in a 30+ channel environment.

The group settled on a test of the ability of seven different methods to measure both broadcast and cable audiences. These included three different telephone recall techniques, some of which had been used successfully to measure radio audiences. Four diary techniques were tested, including two personal diaries and two household diaries, one of which was the standard NSI local market diary.

The standard of accuracy against which the seven test cells were compared was a telephone coincidental; and two-way tuning data furnished by the QUBE system in Columbus was used for validating late-night viewing.

As it turned out, none of the tested techniques was a winner. While some provided better data than the diary for some programming services, none of the test methods offered a significant improvement in accuracy over the standard diary. The standard diary was certainly no standard of accuracy, since it understated cable household audiences by 45 percent.

In retrospect, the CAMS study, even though it failed in its immediate purpose to find a satisfactory measure for local cable audience, did confirm the difficulty of accurately measuring viewing in a multi-channel environment. It's a lesson in humility that we might remember today as we evaluate the people meter experiments.

Ironically, five years after CAMS, local cable retail sales are doing very nicely with—and sometimes without—the benefit of a variety of available research; the most widely available local research is based on the good old household diary; and national advertiser disinterest in cable as a spot medium is almost equalled by that of the cable operator.

An even greater irony is that the concerns we had then about the accuracy of existing methods are now widely held, and it is the national meter-diary system of audience measurement which will soon be replaced with new people meter technology.

All this has been brought about by a virtual explosion in channel capacity, and in the variety of program choices. Ad-supported cable television is one of many program services available to the American viewer. They include the traditional network services, a growing number of independents and even some affiliates carrying syndicated programming, the public broadcasting service, pay cable, pay-per-view, the Saturday night rental video, and yes, even live coverage of the Manchester-Liverpool soccer game if you have your own dish.

The most significant effect of this proliferation of choice has been a decline in the viewing of network programming, and a rise in viewing of all other alternatives.

The implication for audience measurement is obvious: we need a new technology capable of accurately measuring the audiences of *all* the viewing alternatives, not just the three networks in prime time.

Representing an industry that has been severely disadvantaged by the present system of measurement, I certainly look forward to the time when cable television audiences can be evaluated and compared with other television audiences on the same basis.

After all, the needs of the cable industry are relatively simple. Since we are evaluated along with other forms of television for advertising dollars, cable television audiences must be measured in the same way as other audiences. Cost-per-thousand is the currency of television time negotiations, and the system has to rest on a foundation of standardized weights and measures, with no counterfeit nickels.

Last year advertising spent some $15 billion in national television advertising—roughly twice the sum spent on another commodity, coffee. Imagine if you will how consumers would react if they had no assurance that they were getting three-quarters of a pound or a pound and a quarter of coffee. Yes, it would be intolerable; and it would make cable's complex customer-relation problems pale next to what General Foods would face.

As consumers of advertising research, we have no recourse to the Bureau of Standards for our weights and measures. We must set our own standards of validity and reliability for audience research, and we had better do it carefully, for we'll be a long time living with them.

We in the cable business have learned some costly but valuable lessons about the way people interact with their television sets.

Just a few years ago, many of us believed that cable would become a conduit, not only of entertainment, but also of interactive services to the home. We anticipated that people would interact in a new mode with their television sets, that two-way cable would open up new avenues of communication, that transactions such as banking and shopping would become a matter of "touching-in" (rather than the phone-in phenomenon that followed), that vast stores of knowledge would come down to us on our TV screens from that great data bank in the sky, and even that two-way television would restore town hall democracy.

Some of these things may yet come to pass, but the disappointing experiments with interactive teletext, the failure of the home computer to become a common household appliance, the QUBE experience of disappointingly low levels of response (with the notable exception of "Magic Tough," a game show), the decline of the video game fad, the difficulties of pay-per-view—all of these should serve to warn us that the relationship of the viewer to the screen has been stubbornly passive.

The task demanded of today's people meter respondents—pushing buttons to signal a change in viewing behavior—is unrelenting, and carries no reward of its own, as does, say, a channel change to a more entertaining program, or the illumination of a room with the touch of a switch, or the reward a QUBE viewer receives by touching in to "Magic Touch."

Are we running the risk, in Skinnerian terms, of experimental extinction of the conditioned response, button-pushing, by not providing immediate gratification to the viewer? And if we could find a way to do that, would viewing behavior itself be influenced by such reinforcement?

I raise these questions now not to discourage the move to people meters (even interactive ones), but to convey a demand from the cable industry that continuing attention be given to the ways people use technology to interact with the TV screen. We must not be mesmerized into complacency or be intimidated by the substitution of an electronic for a manual diary. We must not confuse technology with validity.

Close monitoring of cooperation rates, in-tab samples, timely compliance to prompts, attrition rates, and the effect of editing rules on the quality of the data will become even more essential as people meter panels age and the number of unreinforced responses to stimuli continues to mount.

These concerns are about the quality of response, or the validity of the people meter data, but we have yet another concern: reliability. This is strictly a bread-and-butter issue about how large the sample has to be. For years, the conventional wisdom has held that "it's as good as it has to be," given the needs of the industry and the constraints of the available dollars.

I'd like to address the matter of needs first. Whose needs are we talking about, anyway? Is it the broadcast networks' need for reasonably stable prime time ratings for women 25–54? Well, a sample of 2000 people meters might satisfy the networks for that purpose, even though their prime time shares have declined for the 90s ten years ago to the low 70s this season.

The question now is, is that good enough? Even for the networks? Prime time now accounts for only 19% of all the viewing, and even the networks have low-rated merchandise in prime time and in other dayparts for sale.

The fragmentation of viewing has created a new need in the market-place—a need for all the players to evaluate with greater precision *all* of the alternative forms of television.

Okay, so who's going to pay? Where will the money come from to support the large samples needed? Well, it may surprise you to learn that the networks are not the only, or even the major, supporters of syndicated research. Advertisers and agencies collectively outspend them, and the newer players—syndicators and the cable networks—have added still more to the pot. It might interest you to know that the combined bill of the cable networks exceeds that of any of the broadcast networks.

So the money is there. And we're going to have to spend it. Because syndicated research has not been good enough. At a time when advertisers have been questioning the value of TV advertising, when there is growing concern about clutter, zapping, zipping, and flipping, it will have to be better than it's ever been to sustain advertiser confidence. Let's make sure that the advertiser—like the consumer of coffee—gets the full measure of value out of every last rating point.

Comments on Chapter 5 by Jonathan Sims (General Foods Corporation)

Dr. Krugman's chapter is thought-provoking; and I would say that he argues persuasively for the need to understand how viewers react and interact with the emerging TV environment (including cable, VCRs, and interactive home services).

If I had to summarize in one word the type of research that Dr. Krugman is advocating, I would say first that it is *motivational* in nature. As Dr. Krugman clearly points out, although the new people meter may accurately tell us who is viewing, it won't assess the quality of viewing, nor how and why people view.

To be sure, advertisers such as General Foods are very interested in the quality of viewership, since TV is often our only means of "one-on-one" salesmanship with our ultimate consumer. In no small way, we believe that television creates an atmosphere not only conducive to short-term sales but also creates long-term equity for our brands—an equity that will insulate us from the vagaries of competitive price cutting and couponing. I think it is therefore fair to say that our salesmanship is enhanced even more through the use of targeted cable programs which emphasize such relevant food issues as health and nutrition. Since we can't always justify such programs on a strict CPM basis, we are implicitly paying for the mind-set of the cable viewer.

I would like to suggest, however, that a company like General Foods is not only concerned with the quality of viewership, or the motivation for viewing. After all, viewers may "approach" TV for seemingly all the wrong reasons, and yet purchase our brands nevertheless. In that case, my company won't worry too much about the viewer's mind-set; we'll simply be glad to make the sale. In this context, our approach to understanding TV viewing is—to borrow a term from the field of psychology—strictly behavioral. And as I think about Dr. Krugman's cogent remarks, there is a lot for the behaviorist to be concerned about.

In Dr. Krugman's introduction, he cites a number of studies which modify, if not refute, the old industry premise that "television selection and viewing is a passive activity." Later on, he notes that basic cable subscribers are "more active in their motivation for using television," and that "segments in this group look for and utilize more channels." Additionally, Dr. Krugman states that the pay cable subscriber, with even more channel options, is "both more directed to television and open to technology than the single pay group." And finally he notes that VCR activity strongly "correlates with cable subscription and other in-home technologies. . . . "

If you put it all together, I think Dr. Krugman has depicted two-thirds of a three-part equation. The missing third is something the networks and advertisers have supplied, and that is clutter.—rampant clutter. The clutter of :60s to :30s, and :30s to :15s. It's the clutter of billboards, program credits, station promos, and station IDs. What we have created, in essence, is a commercial avoidance equation. We have the *motivation* to avoid commercials with the rise in clutter. We have given viewers the *means* to rapidly avoid the clutter by way of remote tuners. And we have provided viewers with the *options* to look elsewhere with the expansion of cable channels and VCR recordings.

Of course, the loss in commercial audience is nothing new for the advertiser. Long before the advent of VCR zipping and zapping, it was (and I trust still is) a biological fact of life that people sometimes have to leave the TV room—especially during the commercial break. I suppose the advertiser wouldn't object to such behavior if it were not for the fact that we have to pay for it. So, while Dr. Krugman advises that we should be "wary of always trying to separate our understanding of commercial viewing from our understanding of program viewing . . . ," I would have to respond that we haven't measured commercial viewing yet; and, as advertisers, we still don't know what we're getting for our money!

Actually, we do know something about what we're *not* getting, at least from VCR viewing. As of February 1987, the A. C. Nielsen Company has been publishing two sets of people meter ratings: one with VCR ascription, and one without. With ascription, the average three-network prime time rating (W25–54) is 12.5—and without ascription, 12.14. That's a 2.96%

ratings gap. From a separate ongoing Nielsen survey, we know that, con-
servatively, 40% of our commercials *which are taped* are either zipped over
or simply never played back.

Multiplying the ratings gap of 2.96% by that 40% figure, gives us an
artificial VCR ratings boost of 1.18%. So essentially, while we're paying
for twelve and one-half rating points per spot, we're actually getting something closer to twelve and one-third rating points. Last year alone, that
cost General Foods over one million dollars in lost prime time impressions.
And our only solace was the curious logic that VCRs somehow offer *bonus*
viewing. Bonus, indeed—for the networks.

And that leads me to my conclusion. Advertisers are no longer losing
commercial audience the old fashioned way. Now, we're losing viewers
still in the room as they zip, zap, flip, and time-shift our commercials.
While the industry haggles and debates over the how and why and where-
fore of the people meter, it will not—in spite of its benefits—measure the
ultimate behavior that advertisers are really after.

And so, I think Dr. Krugman's comments are especially apropos. In his
evaluation of new electronic audiences, he states that "as the capacity to
alter (TV) consumption changes, our existing knowledge . . . of viewing
becomes less relevant, and we need to rethink our assumption about audiences." What better message could there be for the cable industry, as it
searches for a way to quantify *and* sell its most precious asset—its viewers.

Part III

New Horizons

9

In-Home Shopping: Impact of Television Shopping Programs

W. Wayne Talarzyk

Introduction

"Home Shopping Boom Forecast" "Retailing on TV is Exploding" "TV Retail Shows Win Viewers" "Television home shopping may be the hottest invention since the shopping cart" "Home Shopping: TV's Hit of the Season" "Home Shopping: Is it a revolution in retailing—or just a fad?" These and many other headlines and opening lines have proliferated in the popular and business presses during the past year.

Much of the focus has been on the rapid growth of cable television shopping shows. Some authors, however, see the shifting patterns of retailing involving a variety of in-home shopping modes. Much enthusiasm abounds, but in the back of many people's minds there is that nagging reservation—is this the start of a fundamental change in the ways that products are marketed, or is it just an over-hyped aberration? Unfortunately there is not an easy answer.

This chapter is designed to explore in-home shopping in an overview format with specific emphasis on programs offered via both cable systems and broadcast television. To begin, the fairly recent phenomena of cable and broadcast television shopping will be described and evaluated. Then the alternative modes of in-home shopping will be discussed with specific emphasis on videotex. The focus will next shift back to television shopping with a discussion of what has been learned so far. Areas of research issues and opportunities will then be presented. A separate section will provide discussions of possible future scenarios and strategies involving television and other modes of in-home shopping.

Television Shopping Phenomena

Shopping via television is not really a new concept. In some ways its roots can be traced back to the early days of television with the special offers of kitchen gadgets, magazine subscriptions, and the greatest hits of (fill in the blank). Who can forget the K-Tels and the Veg-o-matics? In the 1970s the presentations became a little more professional and the ability to place orders using toll-free numbers facilitated purchases. The stage was set for the development of specialized television shopping programs.

Several versions and formats of television shopping shows were developed and tested in the early 1980s. Most met with limited or non-success. One notable exception, however, was The Home Shopping Club, which initially marketed products by a unique combination of entertainment, product information, and bargain-type, close-out prices. Starting with a single cable television system in Tampa in 1982, a national network was assembled and ready for operation by the middle of 1985.

The operating success and the market potential of television shopping programs became readily recognized when Home Shopping Network went public with its initial stock offering in May of 1986. The rush was on to take advantage of this "new" marketing opportunity.

Major Players

By some estimates more than 40 home shopping television programs are on the market or are being planned for introduction during this year. Some systems, however, have already withdrawn from the market, scaled back their operations, or decided not to enter the increasingly competitive environment. The expected shakeout has begun and many industry observers believe that only a few systems will survive, given the limited market potential. Following, in alphabetical order, are some of the major players as of 1988 based on the estimated number of homes they reach and their potential for expansion and growth. (This is, of necessity, a limited review. For more specific information on these systems and others, along with data and observations on the general area of home shopping via television, please see *BusinessWeek*, December 15, 1986, *Marketing News*, March 13, 1987, and the February 20 and 23, 1987 issues of *USA Today*. Additional information is available from the prospectuses and operating reports of the various companies involved in the field.)

Cable Value Network

Twelve million homes, all cable, 24-hour channel; show hosts present products in random order, emphasis on bargains, somewhat higher-scale items than average, consumer electronics and apparel; owned and operated by C.O.M.B., a closeout liquidator, and a consortium of cable television operators which owns 50% of the network.

Home Shopping Network

Forty million homes, about 40% cable and 60% broadcast; two 24-hour channels with a third channel planned; hosts provide a mixture of urgency and great values in presenting such merchandise as electronic products, jewelry, sporting goods, household products and some apparel in a random order; started with cable television systems and began buying UHF stations in selected markets in the latter half of 1986.

QVC Network

Twelve million homes, about 85% cable, and 15% homes with satellite receivers; 24-hour channel with programs divided into one-hour segments devoted to specific product categories; a public company with some ownership in the hands of cable television operators; features jewelry, appliances, home furnishings, fashion items and some closeout merchandise on "super bargain" program segments; Sears, which selected QVC to carry some of its merchandise lines, has an option to purchase part of the network.

Shop Television Network

Seventeen million homes, some cable, some broadcast; a 24-hour network owned by a Canadian company; focuses on up-to-date products at discounted prices, does not handle discontinued merchandise or overstocks, has some J. C. Penney merchandise lines; uses a segmented approach with some products demonstrated by experts or celebrity hosts, prerecorded segments are mostly 15 minutes in length.

Television Auction Network

Sixty-eight million homes, some cable, some broadcast; this public company has been in operation since 1980 and offers cable and broadcast television systems a one-hour, prerecorded, auction-type of program; features closeouts and off-price merchandise in such categories as shoes and clothing, electronics, collectibles, jewelry, and so forth; a studio audience "bids" on the items up for auction and then home viewers can call in and buy the product at the final bid price.

Telshop

Twenty-five million households, some cable, some broadcast; based in Los Angeles and owned by Financial News Network; this prerecorded program is available to cable and broadcast television systems; the program is a talk show–style sales program with a variety of name brand merchandise and featured vacation packages.

Value Television

Nineteen million homes, mostly broadcast; based in Los Angeles and owned by the parent company of Hanover House catalogues, Lorimar Television, and Fox Television Stations; a one-hour syndicated program operating as a cross between a home-shopping program and a talk show featuring consumer advice from experts and celebrity hosts; features a variety of products from the 21 catalogs produced by Hanover House.

Operating Characteristics

Most of the home shopping services offered over cable and broadcast television operate in similar fashion. The merchandise is presented through a display or demonstration format with appropriate discussion by a show host or celebrity. Usually there is some bantering back and forth between the people on the show along with emphasis on the "great quality" of the product featured and the "real bargain" it represents. Most programs are usually designed to be light, quick-paced, somewhat entertaining, and frequently expressing a sense of urgency to order now before the "chance of a lifetime" passes. Some of the newer programs, especially those featuring current merchandise as opposed to closeouts and overruns, are slower paced with more of a professional style of presentation.

Program viewers purchase merchandise by calling a toll-free number and placing the order with one of the company's operators. The operator, working at a CRT, inputs the relevant customer information along with the numbers of the desired merchandise and the major credit card to which the order will be charged. Merchandise is shipped from the company's fulfillment center, most often via United Parcel Service, and usually arrives at the customer address within seven to ten days. Most shopping shows maintain a customer service department which can be reached via a toll-free telephone number, to help build and maintain customer satisfaction. In most cases, merchandise can be returned within 30 days of purchase for a full refund, including in some instances even the original shipping and handling charges.

Modes of In-Home Shopping

While this chapter emphasizes in-home shopping via special television programs, there are a variety of other modes in which customers can shop at home. Many of these modes trace their origins back to the days of the

Table 9.1
In-Home Shopping Alternatives

Type of Shopping	Primary Mode of Information Presentation	Mode of Order Entry
Door-to-door	Personal	Personal
Party plans	Personal	Personal
Catalogs	Print	Mail/telephone
Direct mail	Print	Mail/telephone
Newspapers	Print	Mail/telephone
Magazines	Print	Mail/telephone
Telephone solicitations	Personal	Telephone
Telephone elicitations	Personal	Telephone
Radio	Radio	Telephone/mail
Cable television	Television	Telephone/mail
Broadcast UHF-VHF	Television	Telephone/mail
Interactive cable	Television	Direct
Videocassette	Television	Telephone/mail
Videodisc	Television	Telephone/mail
Videodisc/computer	Television	Direct
Computer (videotex)	Video display	Direct

Yankee peddler operating out of a wagon. Catalog shopping made its debut as an improved method of bringing broader assortments of merchandise to the rural and remote parts of the United States.

As shown in table 9.1, alternative forms of in-home shopping can be viewed from the perspectives of how the information is presented to the customer and how the customer in turn places an order. For example, with door-to-door sales and party plans, salespeople personally interact with customers to provide information and take orders. With the traditional print mediums (catalogs, direct mail, newspaper, and magazines) the information is presented in printed form with customer feedback via mail or, increasingly, in the form of toll-free telephone calls. The telephone can be a source of information presentation by a seller (solicitation), or means of order entry, or additional seeking of information by a buyer (elicitation).

Television Modes

In terms of television as a mode of presentation, customers can receive information via cable television and broadcast UHF or VHF as discussed earlier, or from an interactive cable system, or through the use of videodiscs or videocassettes using the television screen as a display device. Customers can then place orders by mail or by a toll-free telephone number. In the case of an interactive cable system, they can also place orders back to the cable system's computer through an interactive control unit or hand-held keypad.

Hyde et al. (1987) discuss several organizations which have used video-cassettes to market their products. For example, Murjani International Ltd. experimented with a video catalog to promote its Coca-Cola clothing line; Soloflex offers a videotape on its home workout machine and about one-half of those who request the tape decide to purchase the machine; Royal Silk offers a 30-minute video catalog which features instructions and tips on silk, along with many of the clothing items from its print catalog—the Royal Silk video may be ordered from the catalog for $5.95; Marshall Fields sent a nine-minute videotape to 7,500 residents with VCRs in San Antonio to promote its new retail store there.

In 1981, Sears experimented with putting part of its summer catalog on a laser videodisc and sending it to 1000 customers nationwide. As new compact disc systems are developed and marketed, it may be possible that full-motion video electronic catalogs will evolve. The random access capability of laser discs allow users to go directly to the desired information on the disc rather than being limited to the fast-forward or fast-reverse speeds of videocassettes on VCRs. It is also possible to combine a videodisc, for full-motion visual presentations on a television screen, with a personal computer linked to a videotex system, for current product availability information—along with the ability to order merchandise directly. More will be said about videotex shortly.

In 1977, Warner Cable introduced QUBE, the world's first full-scale interactive cable television system. That system provided a variety of interactive communications services along with traditional television programming. American Express experimented with several shopping programs which allowed customers to order merchandise by pushing the appropriate buttons on their QUBE consoles. The results were less than favorable and the program was discontinued. In fact, consumer acceptance of the total concept of interactive programming was limited. Because of that as well as a number of other factors including budget constraints, Warner has put the interactive capabilities on hold and the system operates today much the same as a traditional cable network.

Videotex

From an international perspective, videotex can be described as the generic name for a new, interactive, mass medium that delivers text and other visual information directly to consumers. The user interacts with the system via a hand-held keypad, push-button console or full alphanumeric keyboard. Desired information is retrieved interactively from a videotex center through telephone lines, cable, or over a regular televison network with text and graphics being displayed on a televison screen or other video device (Widing and Talarzyk, 1982). For additional descriptive information on videotex and related technologies see Tydeman et al. (1982).

In the United States most videotex systems have fallen into two categories: regional systems using dedicated terminals with information provided in color with graphics, and national systems using personal computers with information provided in text-only format. Most of the regional systems (Viewtron in Florida, Gateway in California and Keyfax in Chicago) have been unsuccessful and have withdrawn from the market. Talarzyk (1986) provides some possible explanations of the shortcomings of the systems compared with the more successful national systems.

The three major national systems (CompuServe, owned by H&R Block; Dow Jones News Retrieval, owned by Dow Jones; and The Source, recently sold by Reader's Digest to a venture capital firm) currently have almost 700,000 subscribers. (For more information on these and other videotex activities in North America please see Talarzyk and Holford (1986). In addition to a variety of services such as news, weather and sports information, consumer information, financial and business data, airline and other travel reservations, interactive games, electronic mail and bulletin boards, banking and financial services, and others, most of the videotex service offer some form of in-home electronic shopping.

Comp-U-Card, for example, is available on all three of the major national consumer videotex services. As a pricing and purchasing service, Comp-U-Card allows its members to access information on over 250,000 products via toll-free telephone lines or through in-home videotex services. On-line shoppers can search the data base by product type or features, do comparison shopping and actually place orders for merchandise. Prices are usually 30, 40, or even 50% below suggested retail. In most cases, members of Comp-U-Card, who pay $39 a year for the service, seem to be using the system for pricing information and then using that data to make deals with local retailers.

On CompuServe, subscribers can also shop via the Electronic Mall, which focuses on convenience and the psychological attraction of shopping using the computer rather than trying to underprice retail stores. Developed by L. M. Berry and Company and CompuServe, the Electronic Mall today features over 80 merchants. The Electronic Mall is organized into 16 shopping areas, each one representing a particular product line and group of merchants.

The results of an A. C. Nielson study, as reported in *Sight & Sound Marketing* (1985) showed that the Electronic Mall has better response rates with lower costs than traditional direct marketing methods. During the four-month study an average of 2.1% of the visits to the Mall resulted in

Table 9.2
Characteristics of Electronic Mall Shopper

Sex:	96% male
Marital Status:	64% married
Age:	36 years (average)
Education:	48% college graduates
Household Size:	3.1 people (median)
Occupation:	60% professionals, managers, executives or proprietors
Income:	$44,000 (median)
Computer Use:	10.6 hours per week

a sale. The average direct mail/catalog response rate is around 1.5%. The basic reasons for shopping the Mall included convenience and time savings. A recent profile of the Electronic Mall shopper is presented in table 9.2. The Mall is currently owned exclusively by Compuserve.

Hegedorn (1987) reports that J. C. Penney will be introducing a type of videotex shopping service later this year. The service, called Telaction, will be part of a basic cable television subscriber package, which will allow home shoppers to order products using a touchtone phone. When tuned to the Telaction channel, shoppers choose a product category or merchant from a menu listing of alternatives. Once in a category, consumers are shown number-coded products. Shoppers can request more details about any product and can review their "Shopping Cart" of selections before completing the transaction. Initially the service will reach 125,000 homes in the Chicago area. Depending on consumer and retailer reactions, J. C. Penney may take Telaction to as many as 20 major cities in 1988 and to an additional 40 markets over the next five years.

Trintex, a joint videotex venture between Sears, Roebuck and IBM, recently announced that it was ready to accept advertisers for its expected system trial in 1988. This system should offer increased opportunities for in-home shopping via videotex type technologies.

While videotex has not caught on as rapidly as many industry observers had forecasted, it still represents a significant potential area for the growth of electronic in-home shopping. As the present systems add more services and subscribers, and as new services come to the marketplace, videotex should play a major part in expanding in-home shopping for many households.

Comparison of Shopping Modes

The traditional shopping process model postulates that consumers go through a series of five major steps in a purchasing decison: problem

Table 9.3
Shopping Modes Compared by Steps in the Shopping Process

Shopping Process Model Steps	Modes of Shopping/Buying			
	Store	Catalog	TV Shopping	Videotex
Problem Recognition	***	*	***	*
Search for Alternatives				
Location	*	***	**	***
Personal Service	***	*	*	*
Alternative Evaluation				
Objectivity	*	***	**	***
Availability	*	***	***	***
Assimilation	**	***	*	***
Purchase Decision				
Expediency	***	**	**	***
Ordering Simplicity	***	*	**	***
Outcome				
Fulfillment	***	*	*	*
Post Services	***	**	**	***

* - of less potential value in positive performance of the step
*** - of more potential value in positive performance of the step

recognition, search for alternatives, alternative evaluation, purchase decision and outcome (Engel et al., 1986). To help understand how the alternative methods of shopping relate to the various steps in the shopping process table 9.3 is provided as a frame of reference. This table is based (with permission) upon one provided by Hyde et al. 1987; it adds videotex to the modes they consider.

In this table the greater number of stars implies that the particular mode of shopping is of greater potential value in positive performance of the step. For example, problem recognition is more likely to be enhanced by visiting stores and interacting with sales personnel, and watching television shopping shows with their sense of value and urgency, than by passively skimming through a catalog or going to a videotex system for information.

It should be noted that the process which led to table 9.3 is a highly subjective one and that interested readers are urged to bring their own expertise to bear in interpreting and applying the information. This reference frame, however, should be of value to individuals thinking through the potential of alternative modes of shopping for their product offerings and their present methods of distribution and marketing. Each of the steps will now be discussed via comparisons of the alternative shopping modes.

Problem Recognition

As stated above, experiences in stores with viewing product displays and interaction with store personnel greatly enhance the problem recognition step in the shopping process. Likewise, watching television shopping programs can be very effective in motive arousal and need activation, especially based on the sense of value and urgency conveyed by the programs. The passive nature of most catalog experiences does not often result in the need activating or persuasive power of the other shopping modes. Likewise, since most people go to vidoetex systems for information or to perform some specific transaction there is little potential of problem recognition via this mode of shopping.

For cable television shopping programs to enhance their effectiveness as a shopping medium, the emphasis on problem recognition needs to remain strong. A major part of presenting any product on the shopping shows should be on the types of consumer wants and needs that can be satisfied by the product. This will involve using the strength of this shopping mode with the attentive, receptive mood of the television viewer.

Search for Alternatives

Location, in terms of search for alternatives, is facilitated by the ease of finding merchandise in a catalog and the breadth and depth of information via a videotex system. Likewise, catalogs are immediately accessible at the point of problem recognition, and videotex systems are under the direct control of the user. Stores may not be conveniently located to a consumer and of course the consumer would have to leave home to begin the search/evaluation process. Merchandise may not be offered when desired or needed through a television shopping program, even though the television shopping program is easily and immediately accessible at the point of problem recognition.

Personal service is clearly best when dealing with store personnel. They can usually offer in-depth product information, comparative information, ensemble coordination for apparel, and so forth, if they have been properly trained and motivated to do so. With videotex systems consumers interact with the information base on their own so there is no personal service involved. Similarly, with television shopping programs and catalog shopping the consumer has no direct personal involvement with the organizations unless telephone calls are made.

To improve their relative position in the area of search for alternatives there is little that television shopping programs can do other than offer alternative products at the same time in a given product area. The expanded availability of customer service representatives to provide information over the phone could improve the personal service dimension of alternative search.

Evaluation of Alternatives

With alternative evaluation, objectivity is of highest potential with catalogs and videotex, due to the text nature of the information and the amount available, along with the obvious lack of potential bias from salespeople. Availability of product is generally limited to what the consumer sees on the sales floor of a store, while catalogs and television shopping programs are usually very clear on what sizes, colors, models, and so forth are available. Videotex may offer the greatest potential here because inventories can be updated almost instantly and the consumer can know exactly what is available.

With catalogs and videotex systems consumers have as much time as they want to assimilate the available information. The information must be assimilated quickly in the case of television shopping programs because the product is usually off the air in a few minutes.

Again, well-trained and motivated customer service representatives can facilitate the alternative evaluation for television shopping consumers by being available to answer questions and provide additional information via toll free telephone lines. Using split television screens, television shopping programs could leave selected items on display, along with some product information, while the program hosts go on to other products. This would give consumers more time to think about the product and evaluate it. While this would reduce some of the urgency appeal, the trade-off of additional time to think about the product may be of greater value to some consumer segments.

Purchase Decision

If checkout clerks are available, purchases can be made immediately and simply in most stores. Likewise with videotex systems, the pushing of a few keys on the keyboard can complete a transaction. With catalogs and television shopping shows consumers may get a busy signal when calling and then go through a lot of product and credit card information when ordering, especially with catalog purchases.

To improve the purchasing process, some of the television shopping programs retain relevant information in their computer systems on their regular consumers. This facilitates the ordering of merchandise since the consumer does not have to repeat such information as address, credit card number, and so forth. More efforts need to be placed on improving order entry with specific emphasis on more and better-trained operators, if television shopping is to grow as a shopping mode.

Outcome

Shopping in stores usually means that consumers take their purchases home with them. With the other modes of shopping there is the wait for the merchandise to arrive along with the potential that it may be damaged or lost in transit. Many stores have the potential to provide some post services on a "while you wait" basis. Other modes of shopping have the potential to provide nearly all of the post purchase services that stores offer, but the distance between the consumer and the seller is likely to complicate the process.

Videotex may offer the greatest potential in the area of post-purchase services by electronically directing the consumer to related products or areas of interest. Also, at appropriate times the videotex system may provide reminders about ordering again or about sales or special offers on products of interest to the individual consumer. The ability to store, recall, and deliver such information to individual consumers when they sign onto the system can enhance the personal characteristics of videotex.

Television shopping programs, along with catalog and videotex shopping, are weakest compared to traditional store shopping in the area of order fulfillment. To improve on this relative weakness, the television shopping system operators need to work with the delivery services on reducing the time between order entry and order delivery. This may involve adding warehouse locations around the country or grouping orders together on a geographical basis and delivering to hubs via the fastest shipping modes and then breaking orders down for regional and local delivery.

Obviously, trade-offs must taken into account. Some consumers may be willing to pay more for quicker delivery. Telephone operators, therefore, should have information available so that consumers can decide if they want overnight or two-day delivery in exchange for paying higher prices. Other consumers are likely to be quite willing to wait a little longer and have lower shipping and handling costs.

Summary

A quick perusal of table 9.3 shows that each of the shopping modes offer strengths relative to the other modes. On this selected set of characteristics within the shopping process steps, it is interesting to note that videotex rates quite favorably and is similar to the profile of catalog shopping, but with greater potential in the area of purchase decisions and post-purchase services. If videotex becomes a shopping force within the marketplace it is likely that it will gain its largest initial acceptance among consumers who are currently catalog shoppers. For additional information on videotex and its potential as a mode of retailing see Urbany and Talarzyk (1983) and Waites (1983).

Television Shopping—Learning to Date

A few companies have undertaken proprietary studies, and some consulting firms have prepared private syndicated reports, but little is publicly known about detailed characteristics and behavior of consumer shopping via television programs. Likewise little is known about the performance of the industry to date or its long-run potential. The following points, gathered from the operating reports of publicly held companies, from information presented in newspaper and magazine articles, and from conversations with industry observers, provide a brief overview of what is known currently and publicly about the industry.

1. Since its inception in Tampa, 72% of the 125,000 homes in the area have bought something from Home Shopping Network.
2. Home Shopping Network has an average gross margin of 40% (compared to 28% for the typical discount store), and has a net margin of 10.6% (more than three times the average for traditional retailers).
3. Home Shopping Network sells over 25,000 items each day; 80% of the business is from repeat customers; the average order is around $32 and the average customer places 15 orders per year; 30% of buyers account for about 60% of sales.
4. For its fiscal year ending August 31, 1986, Home Shopping Network reported that 9.8% of the items shipped were returned. In dollar figures the returns amounted to 17.4% of gross sales.
5. Some industry participants are in television home shopping as a defensive strategy—"If we're not there, someone else will be there."
6. Some consumers buy for price, others buy for quality of merchandise—QVC reported that, during the first three weeks, the top 20 sellers among its 160 products included both the least and most expensive items and the least and most discounted items.
7. Jones Intercable did a telephone survey among a small sample of cable television subscribers in small towns in New York and Wisconsin. Results indicated that the most likely television home shoppers were middle-aged (35 to 64) with household incomes of $35,000 or more. Important factors in this type of shopping included convenience and price. Such shoppers were also likely to regularly enter sweepstakes. Other findings on television home shoppers included:
   6%—of cable television subscribers made purchases
   64%—purchase once a month or more
   66%—watch more than one hour of shopping programs per week
   48%—have bought from catalogs in the past six months
   71%—spend more than $20 per purchase
8. Some consumers watch television home shopping programs for entertainment; in addition, for some there is a sense of excitement in not knowing what is coming up next and a concern of switching to another channel and perhaps "missing the bargain of a lifetime."
9. As competition among program providers increases, cable and broad-

cast television operators are obtaining ownership positions in the programs or better shares of sales revenues coming from their areas. When Home Shopping Network started acquiring UHF stations, it agreed to pay cable operators 5% of sales from their zip code areas regardless of how the sale originated.

10. In 1985, measured sales from television home shopping programs were $91 million; such sales reached $450 million in 1986; forecasts for 1987 are in the $2 billion range; projections for 1990 vary from $3 billion to over $6 billion depending on the assumptions made by the prognosticators.

11. For some consumers the novelty of television home shopping may be "wearing off." To help reach more consumers and keep the enthusiasm up, shopping programs are using more celebrity hosts, emphasizing special product categories in certain time slots, and adding games, prizes, and contests to the show format. Home Shopping Network sends its customers "Spendable Kash" (usually valued at $5) on their birthdays to be used for future purchases.

This collection of facts, observations and anecdotal information provides some insights to the television shopping industry as it exists today. Clearly more research and information is needed to objectively analyze this industry, to examine its long-run potential and impact on other in-home and more traditional forms of retailing, and to develop strategies to effectively market this type of retailing on an on-going basis.

Research Issues and Opportunities

As evidenced by the information in the previous section there are still a lot of unknowns and things that must be learned about the television home shopping industry. This part is designed to explore, in an overview format, some of the consumer research and competitive/economic analyses which should be of value to academics, industry observers and practitioners.

Consumer Research

In terms of consumer research needs, there are two broad areas of interest—descriptive and theoretical. From a descriptive perspective it would be advantageous to have more information on the television home shopper such as socio-economic and psychographic characteristics and behavioral patterns. Some key questions include: how do customers who shop from television programs differ from those who use other in-home modes of shopping, or those who patronize various types of traditional retail stores? How satisfied are consumers with their television home shopping experiences? What types of products are they purchasing and how frequently are such purchases made? What are the attitudes toward and preferences for various formats for the shopping programs?

From a theoretical perspective other key issues and questions emerge. For example, are the currently accepted models and theories of consumer behavior and advertising effectiveness still appropriate for messages delivered and products purchased via television home shopping channels? Specifically, how does source credibility, steps in the decision making process, one- and two-sided arguments, information processing, and other communications issues relate to information presented to consumers through such shopping programs?

Competitive/Economic Analyses

Competitive studies which examine the impact of television home shopping on other forms of retailing would be helpful for longer-term retail forecasts. Studies could also evaluate the relative effectiveness of alternative formats for such shopping systems, including basic methods of actually presenting the products to consumers. It would also be interesting to compare sales responses to television home shopping shows offered over cable television systems versus broadcast UHF or VHF stations.

Economic analyses could focus on the potential life cycle for television home shopping systems. Specific studies might address: when is the industry likely to peak in terms of sales volume? At what level of sales is market saturation likely to occur? How many individual shopping channels or shows can be supported by the market? What is it likely to take to be one of the industry survivors? Is there a potential problem with a shortage of traditional merchandise for television home shopping programs (closeouts, liquidations, discontinued products, manufacturer overruns, and so forth)?

Future Scenarios and Strategies

Based on where the television home shopping industry is today and the changing marketing environment in which it operates, what does the future hold? What evolutionary processes will take place in the industry? How should industry members respond to market change, specifically increasing competition? These and related questions are the focus of this section.

Market Segmentation

In most marketing situations today, market segmentation is often viewed as the key to success. This observation is likely to be especially true for the television home shopping industry as it matures. As competition increases and as certain markets reach saturation it will become increasingly imperative that shopping shows and their product offerings be targeted to selected market segments. Fortunately by combining the reach of broadcast television (both UHF and VHF) and the available channels on most cable television systems such market segmentation should possible.

Facilitating Environment

In many ways the business and consumer environment seems quite conducive for in-home shopping in general and television shopping in particular. Talarzyk (1986) outlines some of the areas where this is true. For many organizations it is difficult to find, train, and retain qualified and courteous in-store personnel given prevailing wages and benefits. As a result, many consumers find visiting stores a discouraging experience in terms of seeking and receiving information and sales assistance.

Changing consumer demographics and altered lifestyles are also influencing the in-home shopping market. As more multi-income families emerge, along with the increasing levels of education in society, more families are finding their affluence improving. At the same time, however, there are additional pressures on the amount of time available for shopping.

Many consumers are placing more emphasis on self-fulfillment and instant gratification, both of which can be aided through "do-it-yourself" marketing from the home and the ability to make shopping decisions easily and quickly via some of the emerging technologies. Some of these emerging technologies for in-home shopping can also aid the increasing desire on the part of some consumers for more product information. Information load and consumer decision making (Malhotra, 1982) does need to be considered here, however. Also as members of society become more familiar and comfortable with computers they are likely to be more accepting of videotex type shopping services.

Industry Shake-Out

Given the large number of organizations moving into television shopping shows and the probability of consumer interest waning sometime in the near future, a major industry shakeout seems inevitable. In fact, some of this is already beginning to take place. Some industry observers feel that the market will be able to support only two or three major shopping networks and a limited number of specialty, one- or two-hour syndicated shopping programs. With this in mind, some of the shopping networks and individual shows are going to go by the wayside. Concurrently, appropriate mergers and acquisitions are probable as industry consolidation takes place. It is also likely that relationships between operators of shopping networks and programs and their media (cable television systems and television broadcasters) will become more "equitable."

Emphasis on Marketing

As long as markets are expanding rapidly and competition is minimal, the emphasis on marketing principals can be limited. As the environment changes, however, the marketing of television home shopping shows and their products will become increasingly important. This ties in with the earlier comments on market segmentation and impending industry shakeout.

It seems likely that the shopping shows and networks will have to become more marketing oriented. This will begin with a better understanding of individual markets and their needs, along with a thorough understanding of the competition, all based on sound marketing research. Then it will be followed by improved product offerings targeted to selected market segments, likely advances in order fulfillment and post purchase services, varied pricing strategies including rebates and special promotions, and enhanced advertising efforts to attract consumers to the shopping shows and bring them back on a regular basis.

Revenue Projections

As stated earlier, revenue projections for the television home shopping shows vary greatly based on the optimism and assumptions of the forecaster. Hyde et al. (1987) make what seems to be a reasonable sales projection of around $2.8 billion in 1990 in the United States. This is based on: 94 million households (times) 6% penetration (times) 15 purchases per year (times) $33 average transaction size (equates) $2.8 billion. Based on their projected 1990 sales of $456.7 billion for GAFO (general merchandise, apparel and accessory, furniture and home furnishings and other miscellaneous shopping goods) stores, the total projected volume of television home shopping "can be accommodated within the retail structure without adverse consequences or any other mass appeal mode."

Evolving Show Formats

Based on increasing competition, expanded use of marketing concepts, and a focus on market segmentation, it is likely that formats of television home shopping programs will continue to evolve. As pointed out earlier, many of the new shows have already moved away from the original format of a "strong sales pitch with energetic hosts enthusiastically extolling the great bargain at hand." Different types of merchandise, especially more upscale products, are appearing, along with product experts and celebrity hosts to add varied dimensions to the shows and provide differentiation across competing programs. At the same time some shopping programs are developing game show formats with contests and prizes for both members of the studio audience and home participants. Such evolutions will continue and expand as programs compete to attract and maintain consumer interest and purchases. Once again, the hypothesized "key to success" will be the effective utilization of the concept of market segmentation.

Technology Potential

For two books on marketing and retailing based on emerging technologies the interested reader is referred to Buzzell (1985) and Mascioni (1986). These books provide some interesting and timely perspectives on recent technological developments and their implementations and potentials.

If one takes a longer and more futuristic viewpoint, however, it is intriguing to think about what might be coming that will facilitate consumer interest and participation with in-home shopping technologies. One scenario deals with full-motion-video delivered to the home, in digital format, on demand. This can be a very personalized shopping system, with information brought to the consumer in the desired format at the desired time.

With computer capacity built into a digital television set, with information down-loaded on demand over telephone lines or cable systems, with the information accessed and processed with a hand-held keypad similar to today's remote controls for television sets, consumers of the future may be able to shop worldwide organizations from their home. With computer voice generation and full-motion, three-dimensional computer graphics, consumers may be able to "see" themselves wearing the clothes being offered for sale, using the products being demonstrated and so forth, all with a salesperson "talking" to them personally.

All types of entertainment could also be delivered over such systems in an on-demand format. An interesting perspective is that consumers may learn to use a very sophisticated computer system without even knowing or thinking about it as a computer. It is introduced into their lives as an add-on personal information service delivered as part of a television entertainment system. This scenario could be developed in much greater detail, but hopefully the interested reader will grasp the potential even with this limited description. It is important to point out that much of the technology needed to attain such systems is already available or in experimental modes.

A key caveat remains. Not all consumers will seek, readily adapt to, or even want the type of system just discussed. But some will, and if that market is of sufficient size and economically viable such systems, or variations thereof, are likely to evolve. Will they replace all other forms of retailing and information sources and entertainment? The answer is clearly no! But they will supplement and perhaps serve as primary sources for some consumers. Once again, the key for success for organizations which develop such systems will be their ability to properly and efficiently segment the markets.

Summary

Back in the 1960s a classic article (Doody and Davidson, 1967) was written about the in-home shopping experiences of a couple living in the 1970s. Using a computer they were able to do their shopping at their convenience, with the purchases, even groceries, delivered to their home within hours. Then McNair and May (1978) wrote about the next "revolution of the wheel of retailing," which included many ideas about electronic, in-home retailing.

In many ways both of these articles were on the right track in terms of potential changes in retailing. Also, both were clearly ahead of their time. As all marketers know, consumers do not always do what is probable or what is expected of them.

The question today is what forms of in-home shopping are likely to play major roles in the coming years? Are the television home shopping shows of the present part of the evolution of in-home shopping or are they merely a tangential approach to retailing? Obviously these are not easy questions to evaluate, let alone answer definitively. Only time and the proverbial 20/20 hindsight will yield "answers."

A Japanese businessman once stated what he thought was essential to initial and continued success in doing business in Japan. As cable television system operators, television broadcasters, traditional retailers, and home shopping program developers evaluate trends and potentials of in-home shopping they would be wise to consider his words. "We have to keep one hand on the rudder, which is the present, and the other sketching a map for the future."

10

Home Shopping Programs: How Long Should a Product Be on the Air?

DongHoon Kim

Introduction

"This is a tremendous buy!" asserts the sales personality on the Cable Value Network (CVN). "Just whip out your credit card—any card—and dial the toll-free number. You'll receive your merchandise within ten days in the comfort of your home!" In the meantime, the TV screen displays the product from every angle and the features are demonstrated in detail.

Sound interesting? Apparently a lot of people think so, because home shopping programs have recently taken the TV airwaves by storm. Some even compare it with the intensity and hypnotic power of MTV. Although some may consider it another fad that will quickly disappear, its potential for growth cannot be disputed. Media consultants Paul Kagan Associates (Carmel, California) estimate that the sales for this medium will grow from $450 million in 1986 to $2 billion by the end of 1987 and to $7.2 billion by 1991. Furthermore, *BusinessWeek* predicts that by late 1988 50 million Americans—representing more than 50% of all homes with TV—will be able to shop by video. An electronic marketing consultant goes so far as to say that "it has the potential to change marketing the way airplanes changed the travel industry." According to Jones Intercable, Castro Valley, California, about 6% of cable TV subscribers buy from home shopping services, of which 64% purchase once a month or more.

One of the most well-known and succesful shows is the Home Shopping Network Inc., Clearwater, Florida (HSN). After starting in 1985, HSN made profits of $30 million in its first year of national distribution (by end of August 1986) on sales of $160 million. Furthermore, its stock rose a whopping 800% in 1986. Although it is difficult to estimate how many actually watched the programs, more than 500,000 viewers bought goods from the company in the year ending August 1986. HSN states that its average club member places 15 orders a year at an average price of $32.

The success of HSN has spawned a host of other shows such as CVN (Minneapolis), QVC (Philadelphia), and VTV (New York). Also, retail giants such as Sears, Roebuck and J. C. Penney are scrambling to either enter into exclusive contracts with existing shows to carry their products or to start their own programs. All in all, there seems to be no arguing that this newly born and highly successful industry is making inroads into traditional retailing.

As the competition between similar programs increases, however, such programs must think about several factors that will give them the competitive advantage. These might be the offering of brand name items, competitive pricing, promotion, specialization of the product line in order to target a specific market segment, and convenient distribution. Along with the marketing mix strategies such as those mentioned above, another key factor for success is the efficient use of air time. That is, an important question to be addressed by the producers is how long each product should be presented on the air. In other words, what is the optimal number of products to be presented in a given period of time that will maximize the amount of incoming orders?

If the viewers of such programs are able to comprehend the nature of the product in a very short time and if there is no diminishing of the comprehension rate due to the cluttering of the presentations, the optimal strategy would be to cram as many products as possible within a given period of time. On the other hand, if it requires a long time for viewers to comprehend the nature of the products and if they do not become bored with the long presentation of the same product, it would be optimal to present one product for a long period of time. Obviously, the optimal presentation time must be somewhere in the middle.

This problem is a good example of the classic "newsboy problem." The newsboy problem concerns the decision facing a newspaper boy regarding how many copies of a newspaper he must purchase for stock every morning. He can minimize the risk of having unsold newspapers left at the end of the day—the cost of which he cannot salvage (of course this assumes that the publisher does not refund the leftovers)—by buying only a few newspapers each morning. However, by doing so, he might run out of stock and lose the opportunity to sell more. On the other hand, he can minimize the opportunity loss due to stock-outs by buying a lot of newspapers in the morning. However, this would also increase the chances of losing money on the unsold papers. Thus in making a decision, the newsboy must carefully balance between the risk of losing money due to overstocking and the risk of opportunity loss due to stock-out. In the present case, the producers of home shopping programs must balance between the need to let the viewers comprehend the product versus the need to minimize the chances of viewers becoming bored with the program.

In this chapter, we will attempt to statistically derive an optimal length of presentation time for each product based on a reasonable stochastic model of viewing behavior. Specifically, the model will consider two types of cognitive processes involved in viewing such a program, as well as the time required to achieve each. First, it will consider the time necessary for a given viewer to comprehend the product. Here, "comprehension" would mean not only having sufficient knowledge about the product but also having thought about the necessity, usage occasions, fit with one's lifestyle, etc., to initiate the process of deciding whether to buy the product. Second, it will consider the time it takes for a viewer to become bored from watching the same product being presented for a long time and thus become disenchanted with the program itself.

These two processes in conjunction with one another are closely related to the literature on the effects of message repetition on attitudes and purchase intentions (Sawyer, 1974; Belch, 1982). Most studies in this area show that messages gain in impact for a few exposures but that further exposures—beyond the point of "overlearning"—begin to have a negative effect.

For example, Ray and Sawyer (1971) conducted a laboratory experiment in which a sequence of advertisements were shown on television. The number of exposures to advertisements for different products were varied. Dependent measures were recall, attitude toward brand, and purchase intention. The results showed that exposure to advertising had diminishing returns such that the response curve of recall resembled the "modified exponential curve." Also, Miller (1976) studied the attitudinal and behavioral responses to various numbers of exposures to a poster on a social issue. Subjects were assigned to four exposure groups varying in the number of posters they were exposed to. The results also showed diminishing returns to exposure. This line of research takes the process view that while increasing exposure initially enhances learning (comprehending) and favorable attitudinal affect, subsequent exposures create tedium and negative affect (Berlyne, 1970; Stang, 1975). This leads to an inverted-U curve for repetition impact.

The implication of the results from this line of research is that the optimal presentation time of each product must be long enough to allow the maximum proportion of viewers to comprehend the product, while it must be short enough so that the minimum proportion will become bored and disenchanted.

The chapter will discuss the implications of the basic model and also discuss the factors that can be incorporated into the basic model in order to make it more realistic.

A Stochastic Model of Viewing Behavior

As described above, it is envisioned here that there are two basic events involved in the viewing of shopping programs. One is comprehension of the product and the other is becoming bored with the presentation. These two events can be modeled using a probabilistic modeling framework based on the following assumptions.

First of all, assume that the time until the comprehension event occurs (i.e., a viewer comprehends) is a random variable with a probability distribution function (p.d.f.) f(t) and a cumulative distribution function (C.D.F.) F(t). Also, assume that the time until a viewer becomes bored is also a random variable with a p.d.f. g(t) and a C.D.F. G(t).

Here, some general discussion about probability distributions is in order. The random variable of interest time (t) is obviously a continuous variable ranging from zero to infinity and thus the corresponding distribution functions are continuous functions. A probability distribution function (p.d.f.) is a function that assigns probabilities to values of a random variable where the probabilities are given by the area under the curve. For example, the probability of comprehending by the time $t = 10$ is given by the area under the f(t) curve between $t = 0$ and $t = 10$. A cumulative distribution function represents the probability of the random variable taking on a value less than t. For example, the probability that boredom occurs at or before time $t = 20$ is given by $G(t = 20)$. So $G(t = 20)$ is the area under the g(t) curve between $t = 0$ and $t = 20$.

Second, in our context it is assumed that the time until each event occurs followsexponential distributions with parameters θ for comprehension and μ for getting bored. An example of what exponential distributions look like in general is presented in figure 10.1.

As can be seen from figure 10.1, the parameter determines the shape of the curve. Thus, the two events can be represented by the following equations:

COMPREHENSION:

p.d.f.:	$f(t) = \theta^{-\theta t}$	$t > 0$
C.D.F.:	$F(t) = 1 - e^{-\theta t}$	$t > 0$

BOREDOM:

p.d.f.:	$g(t) = \mu e^{-\mu t}$	$t > 0$
C.D.F.:	$G(t) = 1 - e^{-\mu t}$	$t > 0$

Following the characteristics of exponential distributions, the mean times till comprehension and boredom are $1/\theta$ and $1/\mu$ respectively. Furthermore, the nature of the exponential distribution implies that events of compre-

Figure 10.1
Exponential Distributions
$f(t) = \Theta e^{-\Theta t}$

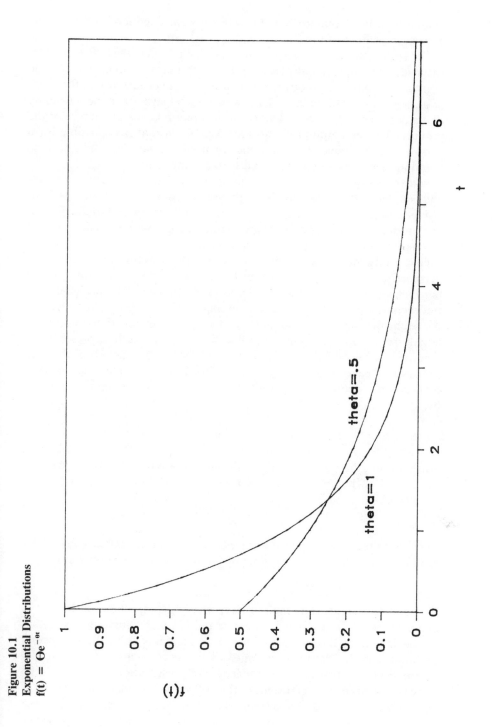

theta=.5

theta=1

f(t)

t

hension and boredom are random with constant likelihoods of occurring at each increment of time.

The third assumption that needs to be made is that these two random variables are independent of each other such that the occurrence of one event (e.g., comprehension) has no bearing on the occurrence of the other (e.g., boredom). This independence assumption leaves open the possibility that a person can get bored before he/she comprehends the nature of the product. This assumption is not unreasonable in that it is possible for a person who has never learned about or used a computer could become bored immediately when presented with a computer.

Fourth, assume that comprehension rates are the same for all products and, similarly, the boredom rates are also the same for all products. This last assumption implies that the optimal length of presentation time for one product will also be optimal for all other products. Thus, each product will be on the air for the same length of time.

Given this model of viewing behavior, the desirable event from the perspective of the producer is that the viewer comprehends the product but that he/she has not become bored in the process. The probability of this event is represented by the joint probability $P(C, {}^{\sim}B)$ where C denotes the event of comprehension and $^{\sim}B$ denotes the event of not becoming bored. Thus we are attempting to find the optimal length of presentation time that maximizes this probability. Let τ denote the length of the presentation of each product. Then, the probability $P^c(\tau)$ that a viewer comprehends the nature of the product by the end of the interval τ is given by:

$$P^c (\tau) = \int_0^\tau f(t)dt = \int_0^\tau \theta e^{-\theta t} dt = 1 - e^{-\theta\tau}$$

Furthermore, the probability $P^{\sim B}(\tau)$ that a viewer does not become bored by the end of the interval τ is given by:

$$P^{\sim B} (\tau) = 1 - \int_0^\tau g(t)dt = 1 - \int_0^\tau \mu e^{-\mu t} dt = e^{-\mu\tau}$$

Then, with the independence assumption, the joint probability $P(C, {}^{\sim}B)$ can be represented by the product of the two individual probabilities:

$$H(\tau) = P^c (\tau) P^{\sim B} (\tau) = [1 - e^{-\theta\tau}] e^{-\mu\tau} \qquad (1)$$

Figure 10.2 presents the graph of $H(\tau)$ when θ (comprehension rate) = 1 and μ (boredom rate) = 0.5. The inverted-U shaped curve indicates that as the length of the presentation time τ increases from 0, the desired probability $P(C, {}^{\sim}B)$ increases but as τ becomes greater, it starts to decrease. So in the first range, as the length of presentation is increased, the increasing risk of boredom is more than offset by the increasing benefit of comprehension. Beyond a certain magnitude of τ (i.e., greater than the

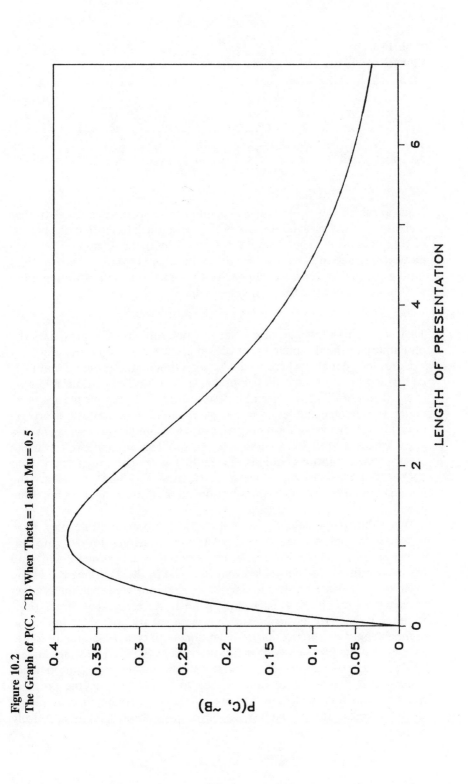

Figure 10.2
The Graph of P(C, ~B) When Theta = 1 and Mu = 0.5

LENGTH OF PRESENTATION

P(C, ~B)

Table 10.1
Optimal τ and P(C, ~B)

				z				
	50	20	10	5	2	1	.5	.2
τ^*	.079	.152	.240	.358	.550	.692	.810	.910
P(C,~B)	.907	.817	.715	.582	.385	.250	.148	.067

point at which the curve is the maximum) the opposite is true—further increases in τ will push up the risk of boredom much faster than the benefit of comprehension. The objective is to find the optimal length τ that will maximize equation (1) above. By differentiating (1) with respect to τ and setting it equal to zero, we can derive the optimal length of presentation τ^* (the derivation is given in the appendix):

$$\tau^* = - [1/\theta] \, Log_e \, [\mu/(\mu + \theta)] \qquad (2)$$

That is, finding the value of τ^* that satisfies equation (2) maximizes the probability of the desirable event of comprehension and no boredom.

Here, let's define z where z equals mean time until becoming bored ($1/\mu$) divided by mean time till comprehension ($1/\theta$). Thus, in our model, z is equal to θ/μ. This is a useful measure in tracking the properties of τ^* under various magnitudes of θ and μ. In a different context, Morrison (1981) has extensively shown the properties of τ^* under various magnitudes of z. Applying Morrison's findings to the problem at hand, we can make several interesting observations. Table 10.1 gives the values for τ^* and P(C, ~B) under various values of z. Note that τ^* here represents the optimal length of presentation as a proportion of mean time till boredom event.

When the comprehension rate is equal to the boredom rate (i.e., $\Theta = \mu$; z = 1), the optimal length of presentation τ^* is equal to .692 (the unit of measurement depends on how the rates θ and μ were measured) and the probability of the desirable event (C, ~B) is .25. This means that the event (C, ~B) occurs only one-quarter of the time even when the product is presented for the optimal length of time. As z becomes larger (i.e., comprehension rate becomes larger relative to the boredom rate), the optimal length as a proportion of mean time until comprehension becomes smaller and the probability of the desired event (C, ~B) becomes larger. This says that as viewers take shorter and shorter times to comprehend, compared to the length of time needed to become bored, the program should devote less and less time to presenting each product, because doing so will increase the probability of the desired event. This is intuitively correct.

Possible Extensions of the Basic Model

Although the model above captures the essence of the problem, several factors can be incorporated into the model to make it even more realistic.

First, in all likelihood, the producers of such shopping programs are not out to maximize the probability given above. Rather, they are probably trying to maximize revenues or profits. If we denote the total length of the program as T, then for a given value of τ (length of each presentation), the number of products that will appear during the entire program is T/τ. So the longer the presentation length of each product, the fewer the number of products that will be presented during the program. Assuming that (i) once viewers achieve the event (C, ~B) (i.e., comprehend the nature of the product and do not become bored in the process), they have a constant probability p of ordering the product, and (ii) all products have equal margins of m, the expected earning per product can be represented as:

$$P[C, \sim B|\tau] * m * p$$

and the total earnings during the program can be represented as:

$$[T/\tau] * P[C, \sim B|\tau] * m * p$$

Here, since m and p are assumed to be constants, they can be omitted from the model without affecting the derived optimal length τ*. Thus, the total profit from a program lasting T time periods is proportional to:

$$H_1(\tau) = [T/\tau] * P[C, \sim B|\tau]$$

Since the revenue factor T/τ is greater when τ is smaller, it will probably drive the optimal length of presentation down so that it might pay in terms of greater total revenue to shorten the optimal τ* and pack more products into the program.

A second factor that can be incorporated into the model is related to the stream of research conducted by Ray and Webb (Ray and Webb, 1976, 1978, 1986; Webb and Ray, 1984) concerning the effect of clutter on advertising effectiveness. This line of research, through a series of laboratory experiments, has shown that increasing clutter of advertisements embedded in a TV program (both by shortening each commercial presented within a given period of time and by increasing the total time devoted to commercial presentation) significantly reduces their effectiveness. Specifically, they found that increasing the clutter of non-program material (e.g., commercials, promotional announcements, public-service messages, etc.) resulted in decreased attention, recall, and positive cognitive responses (Webb and Ray, 1984).

The implication of these findings in the present context is that, although the term T/τ will drive the optimal time spent presenting each product τ* to be smaller such that more products will be introduced within a given period of time, an increase in the number of products presented will probably hinder the comprehension of the viewers. This is because as the viewers are exposed to more and more products in a short period of time, their attention will be adversely affected, and their average comprehension rate will decrease. Specifically, viewers' overall comprehension rate will be greater when each product is on the air for a long period of time, as opposed to when each product is on the air for a short period of time. In the context of the model, the comprehension parameter θ is inversely related to the number of products presented during the program (T/τ) or directly related to length of presentation (τ).

A third extension is related to individual differences. Currently, the implicit assumption is that all viewers have the same rates of comprehension and boredom. This can be relaxed by capturing the heterogeneity through specifying distributions on the parameters themselves. So the rate parameters can be distributed across the population according to some probability distribution.

Whatever the extensions may be, researchers obviously have to make a trade-off between the parsimony of the model and the amount of reality it captures. At present, the model seems to capture the essence of the problem and provide reasonably intuitive results.

Conclusion

This chapter is an attempt to suggest a model describing the viewing behaviors for TV shopping programs, as well as to derive an optimal length of presentation of a product on such programs. Although the model is a quantitative one, the results derived from the model are qualitative in nature. This is because the unobservable processes of comprehension and boredom are very difficult if not impossible to estimate. Nevertheless, extensive behavioral research does exist in this area, and further work will make it more feasible to empirically estimate θ and μ. Meanwhile, practitioners and other experts can probably make educated guesses on at least the proportion $z = \theta/\mu$ if not the parameters themselves. With such guesses, the model can provide insights into the viewing patterns, as well as directional guidance in formulating strategies for production of TV shopping programs.

Although the model was developed in the context of TV shopping programs, it can also be applied to the issue of advertising length. There has been a major debate on the advantages and disadvantages of currently popular 15-second spot commercials. This model can address the issues involved in the debate, and possibly help in deciding under what conditions short commercials will be more effective than traditional-length commercials.

11

The Pay-per-View Experience: Insights from a Field-Experiment

Dean M. Krugman and Terry L. Childers

Introduction

The rise in television services has been dramatic in recent years. Consumers are no longer dependent on viewing commercially supported programming and are approaching television viewing in a different manner. Television services have been termed "The New Television" (Rothe, Harvey, and Michael, 1982) and "The New Media" (Kaatz, 1985). Consumption of programming has been rearranged with a high degree of segmentation (Rothe, Harvey, and Michael, 1982; Webster, 1983; Sparkes, 1983).

The television is now a multichannel monitor that offers more than the traditional network or local programming fare. Consequently, viewing has not remained stable; network shares have declined from a combined 91% in 1976 to 77% in 1986. For homes subscribing to cable television, the total network prime-time share has dropped even more dramatically to 66% (Nielsen, 1986). During 1976–1986, cable penetration rose from 16 to 60%. In the same period, pay cable (e.g., HBO and Showtime) penetration rose from 5 to 25%. VCRs have penetrated over one-third of U.S. households (National Demographics and Lifestyles, 1986).

These new television services represent one aspect of new information technology in marketing. The adoption of computer technology by consumers (Dickerson and Gentry, 1983) represents a companion change in the means by which consumers will search for, evaluate, and purchase new products.

The recent increase in cable television in-home shopping represents another area in which consumers are restructuring the purchase experience and challenging traditional retailing practices—perhaps challenging our understanding of the consumption experience itself. As in-home shopping and purchase technologies become increasingly sophisticated, our understanding of how consumers utilize these technologies lags farther behind.

One new form of information technology that promises to complement as well as enhance existing television technology is interactive cable television (ICT). ICT differs from existing technology in that it allows for two-way transmission of information, transforming television from a passive to an active role in the purchase process. With ICT, consumers can inquire about the availability of products and services through on-line data bases or directly purchase products through cable channels such as the Cable Value Network or Home Shopping Network.

One form of ICT that has recently been introduced is Pay-per-View (PPV) programming. Unlike traditional premium cable channels (e.g., HBO or Showtime) which utilize one-way transmission at a flat monthly fee, PPV utilizes two-way transmission to purchase individual programming, often at a time more consistent with the consumer's schedule.

Because PPV requires individual purchases on a more interactive basis than traditional network/broadcast and cable programming, a study was conducted to gauge the effects of this technology on traditional consumption patterns. In order to more fully examine the impact of this new form of ICT, segments of consumers differing in their prior adoption of television services were asked to evaluate the PPV services. We offer a conceptualization to explain the adoption and utilization of this new fare of media services; and, finally, we report the results of a field experiment designed to assess consumer reactions to this new form of television technology.

Direct Impact on Advertising Decisions

The decline in network viewing has impacted the purchase of broadcast advertising. Almost all of the top 200 brands have started to use some form of national cable advertising. In 1985 advertising revenues were $735 million and 1986 estimates are slightly under $1 billion (Krugman and Rust 1987). Eighty-five percent of these revenues are national.

Marketers recognize that different viewing patterns may occur with regard to new television services. Cable advertisers have been willing to experiment with longer and more directed formats that are more in line with changing viewing patterns (Kaatz, 1985; Jones, Baldwin, and Block, 1986). Radio is now experiencing competition from select cable channels for advertising dollars. Prior to the development of cable, radio was the only major broadcast vehicle offering highly selective markets.

A paucity of good cable audience research data has made it difficult to assess the use of cable advertising. Nielsen has now moved to a totally automated format in order to help remove viewer confusion over the multitude of channel offerings.

There is increased speculation that premium cable services which have not utilized any advertising will be doing so in the near future (Bogart, 1986; Krugman and Barban, 1980). This would allow for a different form of broadcast advertising.

Large Revenues

Cable and pay cable revenues were $8.3 billion in 1986. Those same revenues were $2.2 billion in 1980. Cable revenues are projected to be $13.5 billion by 1990.

What is most intriguing to industry observers is the rapid diffusion of VCRs. Since introduction in 1976, they have reached a penetration of 31%. The largest growth period occurred between 1982–1985. Pay-per-view (PPV), the industry's newest service, is now being viewed as a major revenue source. While revenues were only $40 million in 1985, projections place PPV revenues to reach one billion dollars within the next five years (Trachtenberg, 1985). This may be due to PPV offering viewers the opportunity to purchase programming on an individual basis.

New Forms of Industry Competition

While the market for new television services continues to grow, there is concern that penetration is beginning to mature and stabilize. More sophisticated marketing techniques for product development and promotion are becoming a requisite for success.

Previously, the market had been viewed as traditional broadcasters versus cable-oriented services. This is no longer the case. There is increasing competition within the market for new television services. Pay cable and the VCR industry are beginning to compete for consumer viewing time, entertainment dollars (Trachtenberg, 1985), and available programming (Lachenbruch, 1984; Kaatz, 1985).

Competition is beginning to occur between regular pay cable services and the new PPV services (Childers and Krugman, 1987). Regular pay-services revenues (HBO, Showtime, The Movie Channel, Cinemax, etc.) have stabilized due to competition from VCR rentals. The cable industry is looking to PPV, with its more directed services, as a new factor for improving industry revenues.

Changing Consumption Requires New Study

It is no longer safe to assume that the knowledge generated for traditional television viewing remains valid with regard to new media services. If we accept the premise that audiences are changing, we need greater insight into the selection and viewing process. Researchers investigating new media services have concluded that research is needed to assess changing consumption and to determine its impact. In a study on television audience segmentation, Domzal and Kernan (1983, p. 47) concluded, "The new technology—cable, STV, VCR—requires a richer understanding of audience segmentation since that is the key basis for efficacy."

While studying the use of cable television, Sparkes (1983) concluded that consumer reaction is complex and will require different measures over an extended period of time. Levy (1980, 1983) conducted several studies on the use of VCRs. In examining the role of VCRs and cable television, he concluded that new forms of viewing behavior are occurring (Levy, 1983) and that audiences using a VCR for recording and playback may be more "active" as opposed to "passive" in their approach to television (Levy, 1980).

The above researchers have acknowledged that new forms of consumption are occurring and that it behooves the field to better understand how new media services are utilized. However, there has been only a limited amount of research directed at understanding both the antecedents and consequences of their adoption. In part, this is due to the rapid development of these services and the difficulty of assessing the impact of both single and multiple adoption of this technology.

Conceptualizing New Media Use

Innovativeness and related concepts are judged to be key determinants in the adoption of new television services and related products. Venturesomeness, the willingness to accept risks, has been defined as the salient value of innovativeness (Kirton, 1976; Rogers, 1976; Robertson, 1971).

Ettma (1984) noted that innovativeness is important in the adoption of a videotex service. Studies on pay cable (Krugman and Eckrich, 1982) and home computers (Danko and MacLachlan, 1983) have concluded that venturesomeness is a key attribute in the adoption of those products.

While innovativeness and related concepts have been helpful in understanding the use of new media services, they are limited in explaining how such services fit into consumption patterns. Innovativeness as one antecedent state does not yield a complete understanding of the user interface with new technology (Venkatesh, 1985).

A focus on the consequences of adoption has also been discussed by Robertson (1971), when he noted that some new products only slightly alter existing consumer-use patterns, while others require moderate or dramatic change. The key is the way a new product affects an established pattern of consumption. New products that require slight or moderate change in the existing consumption pattern were termed "continuous" and

Figure 11.1
Individual and Situational Determinants of New Technology Adoption

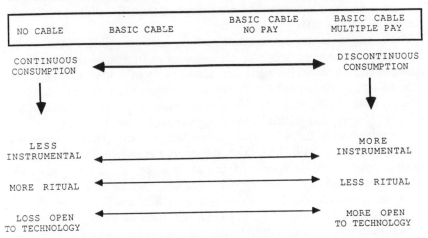

"dynamically continuous." Those requiring a great deal of change are termed "discontinuous." Discontinuous products that require more change on the part of consumers are seen to have a better opportunity to be investigated within the framework of innovativeness (Robertson, 1971; Krugman, 1985). By nature, they require the consumer to establish a new consumption pattern.

The proposed conceptualization depicted in figure 11.1 integrates these issues of characteristics of the individual with the situation accompanying the use of the new technology. Both characteristics of the adopter (resister) of this technology and their existing level of usage of available technology serve to determine reactions to a complementary form of new technology. The framework argues for an interactionist perspective, in which a phenomenon is examined within the context of a preexisting consumption state that is modified as technology is introduced into the household (Beron and Byrne, 1978). Issues such as product complexity, or compatibility of an innovation with existing individual values and experience (Rogers, 1976), rely upon this melding of the nature of the product with individual differences in consumption, in attempting to account for the rate of adoption of new technologies.

Underlying the continuity paradigm is the relationship between existing household technology and the nature of the process accompanying the integration of new technology with existing technology. Households will differ in their adoption of existing television services; thus the adoption of new services should be examined within this context. In proposing an inventory of new diffusion research, Gatignon and Robertson (1985) concluded that research has not been conducted concerning the relationship of new adoption with the individual's existing consumption system: "Future research could contribute by focusing on how an innovation fits into the existing consumption system and inventory patterns." (Gatignon and Robertson, 1985; 854–55).

The focus on existing consumption patterns remains germane to the study of new media services and products. Consumption of such services is usually multiple. Cable television users are more apt to own a VCR than those who do not subscribe to a cable service (Rothe, Harvey, and Michael, 1982; Kaplan, 1978). Pay cable owners are even more disposed to owning a VCR (Harvey and Rothe, 1986; Krugman and Eckrich, 1982).

In a review of 32 empirical studies, conducted in the area of new media services, Krugman (1985) supports the overall framework of continuous to discontinuous consumption of this technology. Basic cable services, which only slightly alter viewing, were characterized to be continuous innovations, because consumers are still watching television but have a greater selection (figure 11.1). Pay cable services, which are bought on a subscription basis and do not have advertising, were judged to be dynamically continuous. Consumers are now directly paying for television without commercial interruptions. Therefore, they are more apt to use television differently than they have in the past. Interactive services requiring new forms of behavior, such as home shopping and banking, were seen as discontinuous because television is performing a vastly different function than providing over-the-air passive entertainment.

The multiple adoption of new television services lends credibility to the idea that consumers possess an overall framework into which they accept or reject new media products and services. Certainly, many of these groups are different merely in the way they are composed according to their "known group" characteristics; that is, nonsubscribers to cable, basic cable subscribers, pay cable subscriber purchasing one service, pay cable subscribers purchasing multiple services.

It is important also to know if consumers falling within these prior consumption categories are different in their overall approach to new media services and their motivations for consumption. At least three areas may prove insightful regarding the way various groups approach new television services, motivations toward using television, openness to technology, and resistance to technology.

Ritualized/Instrumental Television Viewing

Specific motivations for viewing television programming may serve as important anchors for the way individuals utilize new television services. Television research has established the existence of both ritual and instrumental viewing (Rubin, 1983). Ritualized viewing is associated with habit, frequency, and entertainment. Instrumental viewing is more purposeful, directed, and goal seeking.

Directed and active viewing is similar to the notion of high involvement. It has been argued that much mass media content is of a low-involvement nature but that certain media might "boost up" involvement from its typically low level (Greenwald and Leavitt, 1984). Certainly, some of the more selective and interactive new media services *potentially* require more directed or active viewing.

Adoption and Comfort with Technology/Resistance to Technology

It is important to consider how individuals relate to technically oriented products. New media services give the appearance of being technically oriented. Cable terminals have options for multiple input and remote control. Many VCR applications require a good deal of signal and channel adjustment. In cases of delayed VCR recordings, minimum programming skills are necessary. Pay-per-view purchases usually require special codes utilized by a two-way terminal.

Adoption and comfort encompasses but extends beyond television services to include other new technologies. A segment of technology-oriented individuals exists that "requires" technically oriented electronic audio/visual products. They have been identified as technologically advanced families "Taffies" (Yankee Group, 1986). Home computer users are more prone to purchase other new products with a technical orientation (Dickerson and Gentry, 1983). Households active in the use of television technologies are very often more receptive to the use of new technologies (Venkatesh, 1985). Individuals who are comfortable with computers are more likely to use a videotex service such as home shopping or banking (Leadingham, 1984). It is reasonable to conclude that many new television services are viewed by consumers as an extension of technology. Therefore, individuals predisposed to new technology would be more likely to adopt such services.

The literature in this area is pro-innovation and focuses on who is using products (Rogers, 1976); however, there is also a concern for resisters and why they do not use a new technology (Leonard-Barton, 1985). This may be of key importance in beginning to explain the groups that do not elect to purchase or subscribe to new television services. In contrast to the group that is open to new technologies, there is a group that perceives some innovations as too complex. Perceived complexity is considered to be a major obstacle in the adoption of products (Rogers, 1976; Rogers and Shoemaker, 1971).

Sheth (1981) noted habit toward existing products and perceived risks associated with innovations as key reasons why individuals resist innovations. Other research has noted that individuals electing not to subscribe

to cable are satisfied with current programming, or that "television is television" and that new sources were not terribly important (Baldwin and
McVoy, 1983). Thus, a resistance to innovate may be a conscious decision;
it deserves study, along with an examination of consumers open to new
technology adoption.

Hypotheses

The current study focuses on how a media service, pay-per-view (PPV),
is adopted by groups using various levels of related and compatible media
services. PPV is the newest cable service being marketed. With PPV, cable
subscribers select movies on an individual basis, rather than purchasing a
schedule of programming, as in pay cable (i.e., HBO, Showtime). PPV
subscribers must interact with the cable company to order a special program. In this study, they used a two-way decoder box connected to the
television. Subscribers were given their own number codes to order movies.

The underlying purpose of the study is to assess how services are adopted
within the household's *existing* consumption system. The results should
provide insight as to whether groups differing in their past consumption
of television technology possess different motivations for television use and
different orientations toward new media technology, and whether these
motivations and orientations influence the way groups of households assess
the new PPV television service.

Four "known groups" varying in their prior consumption of existing
television services were studied: (1) traditional television users who have
opted not to subscribe to a basic cable service, (2) subscribers to a basic
cable service, (3) subscribers to a basic and one pay cable service, and (4)
subscribers to a basic and multiple pay cable service. The investigation
among these groups allowed a test of the proposed conceptualization regarding motivations for television use and orientations toward technology.

The conceptualization provided indicated a straightforward approach to
how PPV will fit into existing consumption patterns, by relating adop-
ter/resister characteristics with regard to technology and ritualized (habit)
versus instrumental (directed) television viewing. The framework supports
a scheme whereby PPV is differentially posited as a dynamically contin-
uous-to-discontinuous product, and recognizes that consumers in each prior
technology group will evaluate a new media service within their existing
consumption pattern. As discussed, PPV requires individuals to consume
media in a different manner than traditional over-the-air television; since
(1) programs are paid for on an individual basis, (2) the consumer is more
active and interacts with the cable company, and (3) programs are not
interrupted by commercial messages.

Figure 11.2 represents known groups as different segments in a continuum of consumption, and assumes that groups at each end of the continuum

Figure 11.2
Predicted Consumption Continuum for PPV

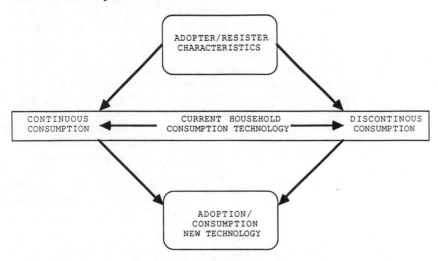

are more diverse than groups in the middle of the continuum. Given the nature of ICT, individuals opting for the new media service, PPV, are more likely to be instrumental or more directed in their motivations toward using television. Individuals who are more routine or ritual-oriented in their motivations toward using television will not be as favorably predisposed toward using pay-per-view.

In general, individuals who resist technology will not be as favorably predisposed to using pay-per-view, whereas individuals who are more open to technology will be favorably predisposed to using pay-per-view. Based upon our interactionist perspective and the contingency-based nature of prior technology adoption, we posit the following hypotheses.

> H1: Prior use of television will impact the way consumers evaluate the PPV service. The known groups—characterized as traditional viewer with no cable, basic cable only, basic cable with one pay service, and basic cable with multiple pay services—will display different structures in the relationship between the antecedent individual factors affecting their reactions to PPV.
>
> H2: Known group affiliation will influence the orientation individuals have toward television and their evaluation of PPV. The orientation should become more divergent as the known groups move from traditional no-cable to cable multiple-pay. The traditional-viewer, no-cable group should be more ritual oriented toward television and the evaluation of PPV. The basic-cable and multiple-pay groups should be more instrumental in their approach to television and the evaluation of PPV.
>
> H3: Openness to technology will be a more important (positive) variable

in the cable one-pay group and cable multiple-pay group when they evaluate PPV.

H4: The number of technologically oriented products owned should be a more important (positive) variable in the cable one-pay group and cable multiple-pay group when they evaluate PPV.

H5: Perceived PPV complexity should be a more important (negative) variable in the traditional no-cable group, and less of a variable in the structure of the basic cable, one-pay, and multiple-pay groups.

H6: Perceived value will be an important variable (positive) in the evaluation of PPV, particularly for the traditional no-cable group.

H7: The more similar PPV is perceived to be to present cable technology, the lower will be its evaluation. This should be a more significant factor among groups with a greater exposure to available services.

To examine these hypotheses, a field experiment was conducted, the results of which are summarized following a description of the study methodology.

Method

Research Design

The PPV technology was a new service to the market that was the focus of the present study; however, basic cable and pay channels were existing services. Since subscribers did not have any experience with the PPV technology, the decision was made to conduct a field experiment. A franchiser in the Minneapolis/St. Paul area agreed to provide support for the experiment.[1] Households were selected from existing subscribers on a random basis according to their previous adoption of cable technology. Nonsubscribers were selected from the records of the franchiser according to those who had previously refused to subscribe to a cable service when first offered by the franchiser. Study participants were contacted and provided the PPV service (not previously offered in this franchise area) for a test trial of three months. Participants were surveyed both prior to their use of the PPV service and following the three-month trial periods. The design was thus a pre/post field experiment with four levels of prior cable service adoption.

Sample

The sampling frame for the study consisted of the records of the local cable franchiser. Based upon these records, subscribers were classified as

1. The authors wish to acknowledge the support and cooperation for this project from Group W Cable.

to whether they had basic cable service only, basic cable service plus one pay channel (e.g., HBO or Showtime), or basic cable plus two or more pay channels. A nonsubscriber list was obtained from sales call records. Each of the four groups was telephoned, the nature of the study was explained, and households were asked to participate for the three-month test period. Households that previously had refused basic cable were offered the additional inducement of free basic cable for the three-month test period. The sample thus consisted of 75 households from each of the four groups.

The 300 households were surveyed about their usage and attitudes toward cable television prior to installing the two-way transmission decoders. Following the test period, participants were again surveyed regarding their reactions to the PPV service, as well as other issues related to the study. Questionnaires regarding the pretest were distributed by installation personnel, and returned directly to the second author at his university address. The follow-up survey was mailed and returned to this address as well. Usable responses to both waves of the survey were received from 99, or 33% of the study participants. Respondents by groups were: no prior cable—17 (23%), basic cable—31 (41%), basic cable plus one pay channel—27 (36%), and basic cable plus multiple pay channels—24 (32%). The low response rates are probably due to the random selection of the participants, serving as a form of experimental mortality, and thus are a limitation of the present research. In spite of this, some insights might be gained by examining the nature of the reactions to the PPV experience.

Procedure

Participants in the field experiment were informed that the study was jointly sponsored by a local university and their cable franchiser. They were informed that the cable franchiser was conducting a test of the new PPV technology, and that their responses would be used as input in the ultimate decision to offer the service at a future date. All households understood that a test of the service was being conducted, and the service would no longer be available following the three-month period. The nonsubscribers were informed that they could, at their option, either maintain the service at cost or discontinue their service.

Materials for the PPV channel were distributed prior to the test period. Households were provided with a booklet of instructions on how to order the service. Additionally, instructions were displayed on the channel for a three-day trial period prior to the actual test, during which time they were allowed to use the system without charge. During the test period a specially prepared program guide was distributed monthly that listed the times at which households could purchase the PPV programming. Due to a limitation in the franchiser's equipment, programming was only available in late afternoon and during the evening. The content of the programming consisted of a variety of movies ranging from westerns to comedy/humor to dramas, and included releases from the prior year. Prices for the movies ranged from $.49 to $3.99 and were listed in the program guide.

Measures

Adoption and Comfort with Technology.

Adoption of technology and media-related services is often found in multiples (Kaplan, 1978; Rothe, Harvey and Michael, 1982; Dickerson and Gentry, 1983; Yankee Group, 1986). Respondents were asked to indicate if they owned or used twelve products associated with electronics and technology: VCR, telephone answering machine, automated bank teller, video TV game, home or personal computer, microwave oven, call waiting/forwarding, compact disc player, cable television, wireless telephone, programmable pocket calculator, and a computer terminal at work.

While adoption and use are important, they give an incomplete picture of the interface with technology (Venkatesh, 1985). Therefore, respondents were also asked to rate how *comfortable* they would be with each of the above technologies. The five-point scale ranged from very comfortable to uncomfortable.

The scale was developed to assess product specific openness for new technologies. This extends previous work which associated comfort with computers with the willingness to use a videotex service (Leadingham, 1984). More general personality variables of innovativeness have also been used to predict the adoption of videotex and other telecommunication services (Ettma, 1984). Venturesomeness, for example, has been associated with the adoption of computers (Danko and MacLachlan, 1983) and the use of pay services (Krugman and Eckrich, 1982).

Ritualized/Instrumental Viewing.

Respondents were also asked to assess their motivations for viewing PPV. Earlier work on television viewing has established the existence of both ritual and instrumental viewing (Rubin, 1983). Ritualized viewing is associated with habit, frequency, and entertainment. Instrumental viewing is more purposeful, directed, and goal seeking. The scales used to determine these attributes were modified to accommodate PPV viewing.

Directed and active viewing is close to the notion of viewing involvement. Certain media might "boost up" involvement from its typically low level (Greenwald and Leavitt, 1984). It has been concluded that newer media services potentially require more directed or active viewing (Krugman, 1985). Therefore, the instrumental/ritual issue appeared germane to the focus of the study.

PPV Reactions.

A number of items assessed specific issues related to PPV. Eight items were used to determine attitudes toward PPV (a = .88). Each included a five-point scale (agree-disagree) with various dimensions of PPV service. Example items included, "PPV doesn't really fill any of my entertainment needs," or "Compared to other forms of television, PPV is a great idea." *PPV Value* was determined by having respondents rate the value of the service from good-to-bad on a five-point scale over the different price levels ($.49, $.99, $1.49, $1.99, $3.99.) *Simplicity* of product use was assessed, since complexity has been a major focal point in innovation research. Products which are perceived as simpler to use have a greater chance to be adopted (Rogers, 1976). Three items relating to the ease of equipment use and entering the purchase code were asked on five-point agree/disagree scales.

PPV service is purchased on an individual basis rather than a subscription service like pay cable. However, there was a concern over the *perceived similarity or differences* between the two. Therefore, subscribers were asked to rate the two services from very similar to very different on a semantic differential-type five-point scale.

Finally, respondents were asked about their *intention* to purchase the PPV service if offered in the future, on a ten-point scale ranging from very likely to very unlikely.

Results

The data were analyzed using canonical correlation analysis. This allowed for a joint interpretation of the two dependent measures (attitude toward PPV and intention to purchase PPV), with respect to the antecedent individual characteristics. Table 11.1 indicates the canonical loadings (structure correlations) for each of the technology groups. The strength of the relationship between the two sets of variables is assessed by the canonical correlations and their respective chi-squares.

Hypothesis 1 is generally supported. Each of the known technology groups presents a different structure among the independent variables. Three of the four groups represent a profile, along the independent variables, that is significantly related to the dependent variables of attitude and intention to purchase PPV. Two groups, "basic cable plus one pay service" and "traditional viewers/no cable" yielded canonical correlations that were significant at p<.05. The canonical correlation for the "basic cable plus multiple pay" group was marginally significant at p<.10. The only group in which the canonical correlation does not provide a significant relationship is for "basic cable only."

Results indicate that hypothesis 2 is supported. Known group affiliation

Table 11.1
Canonical Loadings for Groups Based Upon Prior Adoption of Television Services

Individual Characteristics	Prior Television Service Adoption			
	No Prior Cable Experience (n=17)	Basic Cable Only (n=31)	Basic Cable Plus One Premium Channel (n=27)	Basic Cable Plus Multiple Premium Channels (n=24)
Independent Variables				
Ritualized Viewing Behavior	.39	-	.20	-.63[a]
Instrumental Viewing Behavior	-	-	.29	.30
Openness to Technology	-	-	.33	.55
Number of Products Owned	-	-	.41	-.38
Product Complexity	-.48	-	.23	.27
Perceived Value	.49	-	.52	.33
Product Similarity	.20	-	-	-
Dependent Variables				
Attitude toward PPV	.58	-	.85	.56
Intention to Purchase PPV	.49	-	.18	.56
Canonical Correlation	.79	.61	.66	.65
Chi-square	29.0[c]	20.2[d]	25.4[c]	20.7[b]

[a] entries in cells are canonical loadings (structure correlations)

[b] $p < .10$

[c] $p < .05$

[d] $p > .10$

is strongly associated with the motivations individuals have toward viewing television and their subsequent evaluation of PPV. The differences are more divergent at the ends of the continuum. The "traditional viewer/no cable" group indicates that ritualized viewing is an important factor in the assessment of PPV. This group displays the motive of ritualized viewing with regard to its evaluation of PPV. The reverse is true on the other end on the continuum. Ritualized viewing is a strongly negative factor in the "basic cable plus multiple pay" group.

Instrumental viewing is a positive factor in the "basic cable plus multiple pay" group, but not a factor in the "traditional viewer/no cable group." Instrumental, more active viewing is important to basic cable plus multiple pay users, and ritualized, more habitual viewing is more important to traditional non-cable viewers. The "basic cable plus one pay service" group is a middle ground in this continuum. Both ritualized and instrumental viewing are seen as moderate factors in the structure.

Hypothesis 3 is only partially supported. As expected, openness to technology is an important variable in the structure for the "basic cable plus multiple pay" group, and not a factor in the "traditional viewer no cable" group. However it was anticipated that openness would also be positively correlated with attitudes and intentions in the "basic cable plus one pay" group. This was not the case; in contrast, the canonical loading is negative and thus opposite to the direction predicted. This group is more complex in its evaluation of PPV; however, as demonstrated by the differential loadings for the attitude and intention scales, versus their more uniform loadings for the two groups at the end points of the prior adaption continuum.

Hypothesis 4 was not supported. The number of technically oriented products owned is not associated, in the expected direction, with attitude toward and intention to purchase PPV. Results are not consistent. The variable is negatively associated with the "basic cable plus multiple pay group" and positively associated with the "basic cable plus one pay" group. One explanation may be the nature of products used in this question. Twelve technically oriented products were included, but they ranged from a microwave oven to video-TV games.

Hypothesis 5 is weakly supported. Product complexity is an important factor in the "traditional viewer/no cable" group. As expected, the more complex PPV is perceived to be, the less positively it is evaluated. This same relationship holds for the "basic cable plus multiple pay" group, although not as strongly. This would be expected given their greater openness to new technology. However, the "basic plus one pay" group does not display the expected direction. The greater the perception of complexity, the higher the evaluation of PPV.

Hypothesis 6 is generally supported. Perceived value is an important aspect in the assessment of PPV. Its significance would appear to be greater for the groups demonstrating a lower propensity for adoption of prior cable technology. Value, however, still plays a role among those with multiple adoptions, perhaps reflecting the instrumental nature of their viewing behavior.

Hypothesis 7 does not receive support. The similarity of PPV to existing cable services did not, as predicted, lower the evaluation of PPV. Similarity may have played a minor role in the perceptions of those without prior cable experience, but was not a key factor for this group either.

Discussion

The interactionist perspective used in guiding this research maintained that in order to assess the impact of new forms of existing technology it would be necessary to consider situational factors in addition to the more traditional characteristics of individuals, such as their influence patterns and risk perceptions. The model proposed a relationship between individual characteristics and the degree to which prior technology had been adopted by households. The results provide support for this perspective, and emphasize the need to consider the *interaction* between specific situational factors and individual characteristics when investigating adoption behavior in future research. Through the field experiment, we also found it important to consider the reactions not only of households that had shown various propensities for adoption and use of existing technologies, but also of households that had resisted the adoption of this technology. The integrated study of both forms of behavior is necessary, if we are to broaden our understanding of why individuals both consume and resist the adoption of new technologies.

Results indicate that prior consumption of television technology can be successfully used to develop a framework for explaining why consumers will elect to utilize other new television technologies. The idea of a continuum of consumption is partially justified. The continuum works very well in providing an explanation for groups at the opposite end of the spectrum, and can provide marketers of new media services with a useful segmentation approach.

Specific television motivations of ritual (passive and habit) and instrumental (active and directed) viewing are key determinants in how individuals will evaluate a new television technology. More *general* individual measures relating to technology were not as uniformly successful in developing market segments. Yet there is enough evidence in the openness to technology and product complexity scales to suggest that further work would be of value.

While the scheme of a continuum worked extremely well for the groups most divergent from one another, it did not provide consistent evidence to support and explain the groups in the middle. It is difficult to know why this is the case. However, one reason seems plausible. The group formations along the continuum are distinct with respect to cable usage, but may be arbitrary with respect to their psychological perspective on new technologies. This would explain the large differences between multiple-pay and one-pay groups. The differences between the one-pay and multiple-pay groups were not anticipated; yet clearly these are two very different segments. Thus, support is provided for the proposed continuum, but the exact nature of any sub-groupings and their respective breakpoints deserves further attention. This may also explain why the basic cable-only group was not differentiated along the issues addressed in this study.

In conclusion, if we are to understand the complex nature of adoption behavior, our perspectives and methodologies must continue to advance to reflect these complexities. Various facets of the situation surrounding the adoption context must be considered when relating individual or household factors to a framework useful for predicting the adoption of new technologies. Perceptions of the uniqueness of new technologies, and the role they might serve, must be considered within the context of a household's overall consumption system—particularly with respect to the prior adoption of compatible and complimentary, as well as competing, prior technologies.

The moderating effects of such factors argue for the use of richer frameworks that incorporate contingent relationships and the use of more complex research designs, such as the field experiment utilized in this study. Future research might take advantage of the causal nature of these designs and the need to model complex mediating relationships through such techniques as covariance structure analysis. Through the application of such techniques within the type of framework employed in this research, we stand to gain much insight toward understanding the impact of new technologies on preexisting household consumption behavior.

Bibliography

A. C. Nielsen Company. 1983. Cable Audience Methodology Study. New York: Nielsen Homevideo Index.

A. C. Nielsen Company. 1986. "Television: 1986 Nielsen Report."

Axelrod, Joel N. 1963. "Inducing Moods and Attitudes Toward Products," *Journal of Advertising Research* 3: 19–24.

Baldwin, T., and D. Stevens McVoy. 1983. *Cable Communication*. Englewood Cliffs, N.J.: Prentice-Hall, 254–55.

Banks, Mark, and Alice Gagnard. 1984. "A Comparison of Media Use and Attitudes in Two Suburban Cable Areas of a Large Metropolitan Market." Presented at Association for Education in Journalism and Mass Communication (August).

Barclay, William D., Richard M. Doub, and Lyron T. McMurtrey. 1965. "Recall of TV Commercials by Time and Program Slot." *Journal of Advertising Research* 5: 41–47.

Barry, C. C. 1962. "Commercials and Program Climate: Things We Always Knew 'Til Now." Paper presented at Association of National Advertisers Television Workshop, New York (February).

Batra, R., and M. L. Ray. 1986. "Situational Effects of Advertising Repetition: The Moderating Influence of Motivation, Ability, and Opportunity to Respond." *Journal of Consumer Research* 12: 432–45.

Bechtel, G. G. 1976. *Multidimensional Preference Scaling*. Paris: Mouton & Co.

Becker, Lee B., Sharon Dunwoody, and Sheizaf Rafaeli. 1983. "Cable's Impact on the Use of Other News Media." *Journal of Broadcasting* 27: 127–40.

Belch, G. E. 1982. "The Effects of Television Commercial Repetition on Cognitive Response and Message Acceptance." *Journal of Consumer Research* 9: 56–65.

Bennett, J. F., and W. L. Hays. 1960. "Multidimensional Unfolding: Determining the Dimensionality of Ranked Preference Data." *Psychometrika* 25: 27–43.

Benson, P. H. 1965. "Fitting and Analysing Distribution Curves of Consumer Choice." *Journal of Advertising* 5: 28–34.

Berlyne, D. E. 1970. "Novelty, Complexity, and Hedonic Value." *Perception and Psychophysics* 8: 279–86.

Beron, Robert A., and Don Byrne. 1978. *Social Psychology: Understanding Human Interaction*. Boston: Allyn and Bacon, Inc.

Bogart, Leo. 1956. *The Age of Television: A Study of Viewing Habits and the Impact of Television on American Life*. New York: Ungar.

———. 1986. "Progress in Advertising Research." *Journal of Advertising Research* 26: 11–18.

Boneva, L. I., D. G. Kendall, and I. Stefanov. 1971. "Spline Transformations: Three New Diagnostic Aids for the Statistical Data-Analyst." *Journal of Royal Statistical Society, Series B* 20: 1–70.

Bower, Gordon H., and Paul R. Cohen. 1982. "Emotional Influences in Memory and Thinking: Data and Theory." In Margaret S. Clark and Susan T. Fiske (Eds.), *Affect and Cognition*, 291–31. Hillsdale, N.J.: Lawrence Erlbaum Associates.

Bower, Robert T. 1985. *The Changing Television Audience in America*. New York: Columbia University Press.

Brockhoff, K., and S. Albers. 1977. "A Procedure for New Product Positioning in Attribute Space." *European Journal of Operations Research* 1: 230–38.

Brown, J. and N. Donthu. 1987. "Spatial Partitioning: Geometrically Aggregative Modeling of Preferences and Market Shares." Georgia Institute of Technology. Working paper.

BusinessWeek. 1986. "The Gold Rush is On." December 15.

Buzzell, Robert D. 1985. *Marketing in an Electronic Age*. Boston: Harvard Business School Press.

Carroll, J. D. 1972. "Individual Differences and Multidimensional Scaling." In A. K. Romney, R. N. Shepard, and S. B. Nerlove (Eds.) *Multidimensional Scaling: Theory and Applications in the Behavioral Sciences* 1. New York: Seminar Press.

Childers, Terry L., and Dean Krugman. 1978. "Choosing Window Width when Estimating a Density." *Biometricks* 65: 1–11.

———. 1987. "Pay-per-view": An Assessment of the Competitive Environment." *Journal of Broadcasting and Electronic Media* 31: 335–42.

———. 1987. "The Consumption of New Television Services." Working paper.

Clancy, Kevin J., and David M. Kweskin. 1971. "TV Commercial Recall Correlates." *Journal of Advertising Research* 11: 18–20.

CONTAM (Committee on Nationwide TV Measurement). 1971. *Television Ratings Revisited*. New York: Television Information Office.

Coombs, C. H. 1952. "A Theory of Psychological Scaling." *Engineering Research Institute Bulletin* 23. Ann Arbor: University of Michigan Press.

———. 1964. *A Theory of Data*. New York: John Wiley.

Cooper, L. G. 1983. "A Review of Multidimensional Scaling in Marketing Research." *Applied Psychological Measurement* 7: 427–50.

Cordell, Warren N., and Henry A. Rahmel. 1962. "Are Nielsen Ratings Affected by Non-cooperation, Conditioning or Response Error?" *Journal of Advertising Research* (September): 45–49.

Crane, Lauren. 1964. "How Product, Appeal, and Program Affect Attitudes Toward Commercials." *Journal of Advertising Research* 4: 15–18.

Danko, William P., and James MacLachlan. 1980. "Density Estimation: Are Theoretical Results Useful in Practice?" In Chakraverti, I. M. (Ed.), *Asymptotic Theory of Statistical Tests and Estimations* 179–203. New York: Academic Press.

———. 1983. "Research to Accelerate the Diffusion of a New Invention." *Journal of Advertising Research* 23: 39–43.

DeSarbo, W. S., and D. Hoffman. 1986. "Simple and Weighted Unfolding Threshold Models for the Spatial Representation of Binary Choice Data." *Applied Psychological Measurement*. Forthcoming.

Dickerson, Mary D., and James Gentry. 1983. "Characteristics of Adopters and Nonadopters of Home Computers." *Journal of Consumer Research* 10: 225–33.

DMB&B. 1986. *Media Insights, New Electronic Media*. D'Arcy Masius Benton and Bowles.

Domzal, Teresa, and Jerome Kernan. 1983. "Television Audience Segmentation According to Need Gratification." *Journal of Advertising Research* 23: 37–49.

Donthu, N. 1986. "Flexible Ideal Point Mapping and Product Positioning." Unpublished doctoral dissertation, University of Texas at Austin.

Donthu, N., Roland T. Rust, and James Lynch. 1987. "Flexible Ideal Point Densities for Product Positioning." Georgia Institute of Technology. Working paper.

Donthu, N., and R. T. Rust. 1987. "Estimating Consumer Densities Using Kernel Density Estimation." Georgia Institute of Technology. Working paper.

Donthu, Naveen, and Roland Rust. 1988. "Flexible Ideal Point Densities for Product Positioning." Unpublished manuscript.

Doody, Alton F., and William R. Davidson. 1967. "Next Revolution in Retailing." *Harvard Business Review* (May–June): 5+.

Ehrenberg, A. S. C. 1962. "A Comparison of TV Audience Pleasures." *Journal of Advertising Research*. 11–16.

Engel, James F., Roger D. Blackwell, and Paul W. Miniard. 1986. *Consumer Behavior*. Fifth edition. Chicago: The Dryden Press.

Epanechnikov, V. A. 1969. "Nonparametric Estimation of a Multivariate Probability Density." *Theory of Probability and Applications* 14: 153–58.

Ettma, J. 1984. "Three Phases in the Creation of Information Inequities: An Empirical Assessment of a Prototype Videotext System." *Journal of Broadcasting* 28: 383–95.

Eyes on Television. 1980. Conducted by Audits and Surveys Inc., sponsored by *Newsweek*.

Fryer, M. J. 1977. "A Review of Some Non-Parametric Methods of Density Estimation." *Journal of Institute of Mathematical Applications* 18: 371–80.

Gallup and Associates. 1986. "Gallup Youth Survey."

Gatignon, Hubert, and Thomas Robertson. 1985. "A Propositional Inventory for New Diffusion Research." *Journal of Consumer Research* 11: 849–67.

Gavish, B., D. Horsky, and K. Srikanth. 1983. "An Approach to the Optimal Positioning of A New Product." *Management Science* 29: 1277–97.

Green, P. E. 1970. "Measurement and Data Analysis." *Journal of Marketing* 34: 15–17.

Green, P. E., and F. J. Carmone. 1969. "Multidimensional Scaling: An Introduction and Comparison of Nonfolding Techniques." *Journal of Marketing Research* 6: 330–41.

Green, P. E., and F. J. Carmone. 1970. *Multidimensional Scaling and Related Techniques in Marketing Analysis*. Boston: Allyn and Bacon.

Green, P. E., and F. J. Carmone. 1972. "Marketing Research Applications of Nonmetric Multidimensional Scaling Methods." In A. K. Romney, R. N. Shepard, and S. B. Nerlove (Eds.) Multidimensional Scaling: *Theory and Applications in the Behavioral Sciences* 2. New York: Seminar Press.

Green, P. E., and Y. Wind. 1973. *Multiattribute Decisions in Marketing: A Measurement Approach*. Hinsdale, Ill.: Dryden Press.

Greenwald, Anthony, and Clark Leavitt. 1984. "Audience Involvement in Advertising: Four Levels." *Journal of Consumer Research* 11: 90–95.

Hair, J. F., Jr., R. E. Anderson, R. L. Tatham, and B. J. Gradlowsky. 1979. *Multivariate Data Analysis*. Tulsa, Okla.: Petroleum Publishing Company.

Harvey, M. G., and J. T. Rothe. 1986. "Video Cassette Recorders: Their Impact on Viewers and Advertisers." *Journal of Advertising Research* 25: 19–27.

Hauser, J. R., and P. Simmie. 1981. "Profit Maximizing Perceptual Positions: An Integrated Theory for the Selection of Product Features and Price." *Management Science* 27: 33–56.

Heeter, Carrie, and Bradley S. Greenberg. 1985. "Cable and Program Choice." In D. Zillmann and J. Bryant (Eds.) *Selective Exposure to Communication*. Hillsdale, N.J.: Lawrence Erlbaum.

Heeter, Carrie, and Bradley S. Greenberg. 1985. "Profiling the Zappers." *Journal of Advertising Research* 25 (No. 2): 15–19.

Hegedorn, Ann. 1987. "Penney's Profit Climbed 13% In 4th Quarter." *The Wall Street Journal* (February 19): 4.

Hoffman, Donna L. 1984. "A Multivariate Analysis of Audience Attitudes and Behaviors During Television Viewing." Unpublished doctoral dissertation, University of North Carolina.

Home Testing Institute, Inc. 1963. "Must Reading About HTI and TVQ." In-house Report No. 22 (March).

Hooper, C. 1966. "Non-Response on TV Meter Panels." *Journal of Advertising Research*: 25–27.

Horn, Martin I., and William J. McEwen. 1977. "The Effect of Program Context on Commercial Performance." *Journal of Advertising* 6: 23–27.

Hyde, Linda L., Cathy S. Dybdahl, and William R. Davidson. 1987. "TV Home Shopping: Opportunities/Constraints." Special publication of Management Horizon, a division of Price Waterhouse (February).

Isen, Alice M., Barbara Means, Robert Patrick, and Gary Nowicki. 1982. "Some Factors Influencing Decision-Making Strategy and Risk Taking." In Margaret S. Clark and Susan T. Fiske (Eds.) *Affect and Cognition* 243–61. Hillsdale, N.J.: Lawrence Erlbaum Associates.

J. Walter Thompson USA. 1986. "Flippers: Changes in the Way Americans Watch TV." 10.

James, Watson S. 1983. "The New Electronic Media: An Overview." *Journal of Advertising Research* 23 (No. 4): 33–37.

Jones, Kensinger, Thomas F. Baldwin, and Martin P. Block. 1986. *Cable Advertising: New Ways to New Business.* Englewood Cliffs, N.J.: Prentice-Hall.

Kaatz, R. B. 1985. *Cable Advertisers Handbook.* Lincolnwood, Illinois: Crain Books.

Kamakura, W. A., and R. K. Srivastava. "An Ideal-Point Probabilistic Choice Model: Accounting For Individual Differences." *Marketing Science.* Forthcoming.

Kaplan, Stewart. 1978. "The Impact of Cable Television Services on the Use of Competing Media." *Journal of Broadcasting* 22 (No. 2): 18–25.

Kennedy, John R. 1971. "How Program Environment Affects TV Commercials." *Journal of Advertising Research* 11: 33–38.

Keon, J. W. 1983. "Product Positioning: TRINODAL Mapping of Brand Images, Ad Images, and Consumer Preferences." *Journal of Marketing Research* 20: 380–92.

Kirton, Michael. 1976. "Adapters and Innovators: A Description and Measure." *Journal of Applied Psychology* 61: 622–29.

Krugman, Dean M. 1985. "Evaluating the Audiences of the New Media." *Journal of Advertising* 14: 21–7.

———. 1986. "The VCR User Report." *National Demographics and Lifestyles* (Research Rep. 2: 13). Denver, Colo.

Krugman, Dean M., and Arnold Barban. 1978. "Advertising and Cable Television: A Realistic Assessment." *Journal of Advertising* 7: 4–8.

———. 1980. "Wiring of Urban Areas, Use of Spots on Pay Channels to Share Cable Advertising's Future." *Marketing News* (November 26, 1982).

Krugman, Dean M., and Don Eckrich. 1982. "Differences Between Cable and Pay Cable Viewers." *Journal of Advertising Research* 22: 23–29.

Krugman, Dean M., and Roland T. Rust. 1987. "The Impact of Cable Penetration on Network Viewing and Telecommunication Industry Advertising Revenues." Unpublished working paper.

Krugman, Herbert E. 1983. "Television Program Interest and Commercial Interruption." *Journal of Advertising Research* 23: 21–23.

Kruskal, J. B. 1964. "Multidimensional Scaling by Optimizing Goodness-of-Fit To a Nonmetric Hypothesis." *Psychometrika* 29: 1–28.

Kuehn, A. A., and R. L. Day. 1962. "Strategy for Product Quality." *Harvard Business Review* 50: 100–10.

Lachenbruch, D. 1984. "VCRs: The Hottest Thing Since Television." *Channels* 4: 6–8.

Lancaster, Kent M., Peggy J. Kreshel, and Joya R. Harris. 1986. "Estimating the Impact of Advertising Media Plans: Media Executives Describe Weighting and Timing Factors." *Journal of Advertising* 15 (No. 3): 21–29.

Leadingham, John A. 1984. "Are Consumers Ready for the Information Age?" *Journal of Advertising Research* 24: 31–7.

Leonard-Barton, Dorothy. 1985. "Experts as Negative Opinion Leaders in the Diffusion of a Technological Innovation." *Journal of Consumer Research* 11: 914–26.

Levine, T. E. 1979. "Joint Space Analysis of "Pick Any" Data: Analysis of Choice from an Unrestricted Set of Alternatives." *Psychometrika* 44: 85–92.

Levy, Mark R. 1980. "Program Playback Preferences in VCR Households." *Journal of Broadcasting* 24: 327–36.

Levy, Mark R. 1983. "The Time Shifting Use of Video Recorders." *Journal of Broadcasting* 27: 264.

Levy, Mark B. 1981. "Home Video Recorders and Time Shifting." *Journal of Broadcasting* 58 (No. 4): 401–4.

Luce, R. D. 1959. *Individual Choice Behavior*. New York: Wiley.

Mackay, D. B., and R. W. Olshavsky. 1975. "Cognitive Maps of Retail Locations: An Investigation of Some Basic Issues." *Journal of Consumer Research* 2: 197–205.

Malhotra, Naresh K. 1982. "Information Load and Consumer Decision Making." *Journal of Consumer Research* 8: 419–30.

Marketing News. 1987. March 13.

Mascioni, Michael. 1986. *Electronic Retailing*. Knowledge Industry Publication, Inc.

McNair, Malcolm P., and Eleanor G. May. 1978. "The Next Revolution of the Retailing Wheel." *Harvard Business Review* 56: 81–91.

Metzger, Gale D. 1983. "Cable Television Audiences." *Journal of Advertising Research* 23: 41–47.

Miller, R. L. 1976. "Mere Exposure, Psychological Reactance and Attitude Change." *Public Opinion Quarterly* 40: 229–33.

Morrison, D. L. 1981. "A Stochastic Model for Test-Retest Correlations." *Psychometrika* 46: 143–51.

Murphy, John H., Isabella C. M. Cunningham, and Gary B. Wilcox. 1979. "The Impact of Program Environment on Recall of Humorous Television Commercials." *Journal of Advertising Research* 8: 17–21.

National Demographics and Lifestyle. 1986. "National Profile, Cable Viewers." Denver, Colorado.

Neidell, L. A. 1969. "The Use of Nonmetric Multidimensional Scaling in Marketing Analysis." *Journal of Marketing* 33: 37–43.

Newspaper Advertising Bureaus, Inc. 1981. "Trends in TV Commercial Recall, 1965–81: A Report on Three Surveys of Prime-Time Network Viewers" (June).

Nuttall, C. G. F. 1962. "TV Commercial Audiences in the United Kingdom." *Journal of Advertising Research* 2: 19–28.

———. 1962. "On the Estimation of Probability Density Function and Market Opportunities." *Journal of Contemporary Business* 4: 35–67.

Parzen, E. 1979. "Non-Parametric Statistical Data Modeling." *Journal of the American Statistical Association* 74: 105–21.

Pessemier, E. A. 1975. "Market Structure Analysis of New Product and Market Opportunities." *Journal of Contemporary Business*, Vol. 4, 35–67.

Petty, Richard E., and John Cacioppo. 1979. "Issue Involvement Can Increase or Decrease Persuasion by Enhancing Message-Relevant Cognitive Responses." *Journal of Personality and Social Psychology* 37: 1915–26.

Poltrack, David. Quote taken from "People Meters." *The New Yorker* (March 1987): 25.

Ramsey, J. O. 1977. "Maximum Likelihood Estimation in Multidimensional Scaling." *Psychometrika* 42: 241–66.

Rapaport, David. 1961. *Emotions and Memory*. New York: Science Editions Inc.

———. 1956. "Remarks on Some Non-Parametric Estimates of a Density Function." *Annals of Mathematical Statistics* 27: 832–37.

Ray, Michael L., and A. G. Sawyer. 1971. "Repetition in Media Models: A Laboratory Technique." *Journal of Marketing Research* 8: 20–29.

Ray, Michael L., and P. H. Webb. 1976. "Research on the Effects of Television Clutter: Dealing With a Difficult Environment." Report No. 76-102. Cambridge, Mass.: Marketing Science Institute.

———. 1978. "Advertising Effectiveness in a Crowded Television Environment." Report No. 78-113. Cambridge, Mass.: Marketing Science Institute.

———. 1986. "Three Prescriptions for Clutter." *Journal of Advertising Research* 16: 69–77.

Richardson, M. W. 1938. "Multidimensional Psychophysics." *Psychological Bulletin* 35, 659–60 (Abstract).

Robertson, Thomas. 1971. *Innovative Behavior and Communication*. New York: Holt, Rinehart, Winston.

Robertson, Thomas S., and Hubert Gatingnon. 1986. "Competitive Effects on Technology Diffusion." *Journal of Marketing* 50 (July): 1–12.

Rogers, Everett M. 1976. "New Product Adoption and Diffusion." *Journal of Consumer Research* 2: 290–301.

Rogers, E. M., and F. F. Shoemaker. 1971. *Communication of Innovation*. New York: The Free Press.

Rosenblatt, M. 1971. "Curve Estimates." *Annals of Mathematical Statistics* 42: 1815–42.

Rothe, James T., Michael G. Harvey, and George C. Michael. 1982. "Perspectives on the New Television." *Business Horizons* 25: 55–62.

Rubin, Alan M. 1983. "Television Uses and Gratifications: The Interactions of Viewing Patterns and Motivations." *Journal of Broadcasting* 27: 37–51.

Rust, R. T. 1987. "Flexible Regression." The University of Texas at Austin. Working paper.

Rust, R., and J. Brown. 1986. "Estimation and Comparison of Market Areas." *Journal of Retailing*, Winter, 410–30.

Rust, Roland, and Naveen Donthu. 1988. "Programming and Positioning Strategy for Cable Television Networks." *Journal of Advertising*. Forthcoming.

Ryans, A. B. 1974. "Estimating Consumer Preferences For a New Durable Brand In An Established Product Class." *Journal of Marketing Research* 11: 434–43.

Sawyer, A. G. 1974. "The Effects of Repetition: Conclusions and Suggestions about Experimental Laboratory Research." In G. D. Hughes and M. L. Ray (Eds.) *Buyer/Consumer Information Processing* 190–219. Chapel Hill: University of North Carolina Press.

Schonmann, P. H., and M. M. Wang. 1972. "An Individual Difference Model for the Multidimensional Analysis of Preference Data." *Psychometrika* 37: 275–309.

Schwerin, H. A. 1958. "Do Today's Programs Provide the Wrong Commercial Climate?" *Television Magazine* 15: 44–47.

———. 1960. "Program-Commercial Compatibility: A Summary of SRC's Findings on the Relationship that Exists between the Television Commercial and Its Environment." *Schwerin Research Corporation Bulletin* 8.

Shepard, Roger. 1962. "The Analysis of Proximities: MDS With an Unknown Distance Function." I and II, *Psychometrika* 27, 125–40 and 219–46.

Shepard, R. D. 1962. "Metric Structures in Ordinal Data." *Journal of Mathematical Psychology* 3: 287–315.

Sheth, Jagdish. 1981. "Psychology of Innovation Resistance: The Less Developed Concept (LDC) In Diffusion Research." *Research in Marketing* 4: 273–82.

Shocker, A. D., and V. Srinivasan. 1974. "A Consumer Based Methodology for Introduction of New Products Ideas." *Management Science* 20: 921–37.

Siebert, Donald E. 1978. "The Effect of Program Content on Commercial Recall." Paper presented at the A.N.A. Television Workshop, New York (March).

Sight & Sound Marketing. 1985. "Videotex Becomes Ad Medium as Home Computers Get More Use." *Sight & Sound Marketing* (May): 3+.

Silverman, B. W. 1986. *Density Estimation for Data Analysis and Statistics*. New York: Chapman and Hall.

Smith, Donald C. 1956. "Television Program Selection, Liking for Television Programs, and Levels of Attention Given to Television Programs by Housewives." R lio-Television Audience Studies, New Series No. 3. Departmei f Speech, Ohio State University.

Soldow, Gary F., ¿ ـu Victor Principe. 1981. "Response to Commercials as a Function of Program Context." *Journal of Advertising Research* 21: 59–65.

Sparkes, Vernone M. 1983. "Public Perception of and Reaction to Multi-Channel Cable Television Service." *Journal of Broadcasting* 27: 163–75.

Srinivasan, V., and A. D. Shocker. "Linear Programming Techniques for Multidimensional Analysis of Preferences." *Psychometrika* 38: 337–69.

Standard and Poors. 1986. "Industry Surveys" 154 (No. 40): Sec. 1, M22–M26.

Stang, D. J. 1975. "The Effects of Mere Exposure on Learning and Affect." *Journal of Personality and Social Psychology* 31: 7–13.

Stanton, J., and J. Lowenhar. 1977. "Perceptual Mapping of Consumer Products and Television Shows." *Journal of Advertising Research* 6: 16–22.

Steiner, G. A. 1966. "The People Look at Commercials: A Study of Audience Behavior." *Journal of Business* 39.

Strack, Fritz, and Leonard Martin. 1987. "Thinking, Judging, and Communicating: A Process Account of Context Effects in Attitude Surveys." In Hippler, Hans. J., Norbert Schwarz, and Seymour Sudman. *Social Information Processing and Survey Methodology*. New York: Springer.

Sudman, Seymour, and Robert Ferber. 1979. *Consumer Panels* 58–61. Chicago: American Marketing Association.

Takane, Y., F. W. Young, and J. de Leeuw. 1977. "Nonmetric Individual Differences Multidimensional Scaling: An Alternating Least Squares Method with Optimal Scaling Features." *Psychometrika* 42: 7–67.

Talarzyk, W. Wayne. 1986. "Electronic Retailing in the United States: Trends and

Potentials." Proceedings of the EPos/EFPTos Conference, Barbican Centre, London (October 8): K1–K11.

Talarzyk, W. Wayne, and Elyzabeth Holford. 1986. "Videotex Project Reviews V." Working Paper Series WPS 86–129. College of Business: Ohio State University.

Television Audience Assessment, Inc. 1983. *The Audience Rates Television*. Cambridge, Mass.: Television Audience Assessment, Inc.

———. 1984a. *Commercial Effectiveness and Viewers' Involvement with Television Programs: A Literature Review*. Cambridge, Mass.: Television Audience Assessment, Inc.

———. 1984b. *Program Impact and Program Appeal: Qualitative Ratings and Commercial Effectiveness*. Cambridge, Mass.: Television Audience Assessment, Inc.

Television Digest. 1985. *Cable and Services Volume, TV and Cable Factbook* 54.

Torgerson, W. S. 1958. *Theory and Methods of Scaling*. New York: John Wiley.

Trachtenberg, J. A. 1985. "Here We Go Again." *Forbes* (August 26): 108–14.

Turner, R. E. 1971. "Market Measures From Salesmen: A Multidimensional Scaling Approach." *Journal of Marketing Research* 8: 165–72.

Twyman, W.A. 1974. "Setting TV Advertising in Context." Research Bureau Limited. London.

Tydeman, John et al. 1982. *Teletext and Videotex in the United States—Market Potential, Technology, Public Policy Issues*. New York: McGraw Hill.

Urban, Glen. 1975. "Perceptor: A Model for Product Positioning." *Management Science* 21, 858–71.

Urban, Joel, and W. Wayne Talarzyk. 1983. "Videotex: Implications for Retailing." *Journal of Retailing* 59: 76–92.

USA Today. 1987. February 20, 23.

Venkatesh, Alladi. 1985. "A Conceptualization of the Household/Technology Interaction." Proceedings of the Association of Consumer Research 12: 189–94.

"Video Forecast" 1985. *TV Digest* 24 (No. 35): 17.

Waites, William. 1983. "Videotex: A Complement to Traditional Media, Retailing." *Direct Marketing* (October): 150–68.

Webb, P. H., and M. L. Ray. 1984. "Effects of TV Clutter." *Journal of Advertising Research* 14: 19–24.

Webster, James. 1983. "The Impact of Cable and Pay Cable Television of Local Station Audiences." *Journal of Broadcasting* 27: 119–25.

Webster, James G. 1986. "Audience Behavior in the New Media Environment." *Journal of Communication* 36: 77–91.

Weyman, E. J. 1972. "Nonparametric Probability Density Estimation: A Summary of Available Methods." *Technometrics* 14: 533–46.

Widing, Robert E., and W. Wayne Talarzyk. 1982. "Introduction to and Issues with Videotex: Implications for Marketing." Working Paper Series. WPS 82–16. College of Business: Ohio State University.

Williams, Fredrick. 1987. *Technology and Communication Behavior* 155–58. Belmont, Calif.: Wadsworth Publishing.

Wind, Y. 1978. "Issues and Advancements in Segmentation Research." *Journal of Marketing Research* 15: 317–37.

Woodroofe, M. 1970. "On Choosing a Delta-Sequence." *Annals of Mathematical Statistics* 41: 1665–71.

Yankee Group. 1986. "Technologically Advanced Families Grow in Size and Importance" (January 9). (Available from The Yankee Group, 89 Broad Street, 14th Floor, Boston, MA 02110).

Yorke, David A., and Philip J. Kitchen. 1985. "Channel Flickers and Video Speeders." *Journal of Advertising Research* 25: 21–25.

Young, G., and A. S. Householder. 1938. "Discussion of a Set of Points in Terms Of Their Mutual Distances." *Psychometrika* 3: 19–22.

Yuspeh, Sonia. 1979. "The Media versus the Message (The Effects of Program Environment on the Performance of Commercials)." Paper presented at the Tenth Attitude Research Conference, American Marketing Association, Hilton Head, S.C. (February 1979).

Zinnes, J. L., and D. B. MacKay. 1983. "Probabilistic Multidimensional Scaling: Complete and Incomplete Data." *Psychometrika* 48: 27–45.

Zufryden, F. 1979. "ZIPMAP—A Zero-One Integer Programming Model for Market Segmentation and Product Positioning." *Journal of Operational Research Society* 30: 63–70.

Index

Contributors

Editors' Note: The institutional affiliations and designations given below were current at the time the conference was held, and may have changed more recently. All biographical notes have been edited for brevity.

RAJEEV BATRA (Ph.D.) is Associate Professor, School of Business Administration, University of Michigan. His research interests cover the consumer processing of advertising, emotional advertising, and repetition and budgeting issues. He was previously a Brand Manager with Chesebrough-Pond's.

WILLIAM BATTINO (MBA) is the senior industry analyst of Coopers and Lybrand's National Information Industry Group, specializing in strategic planning consulting to cable, publishing and information services companies. He leads the Firm's cable television market research studies.

TERRY L. CHILDERS is Associate Professor of Marketing at the Carlson School of Management at the University of Minnesota. Dr. Childers' research interests center on marketing communications, and the relationships between memory processes and the visual versus verbal components of print advertisements.

JAMES A. DePALMA is a general practice partner in the New York office of Coopers and Lybrand, and is a leader of the firm's Infocom group, for which he has analyzed the cable industry extensively. He is a certified public accountant, with over 15 years of broad-based experience in public accounting.

NAVEEN DONTHU (Ph.D.) is Assistant Professor at the College of Management, Georgia Institute of Technology. His research interests are in the area of product planning and market area analysis.

RASHI GLAZER (Ph.D.) is Associate Professor at the Columbia Business School. His research focuses on decision-making, marketing strategy, and the adoption of new technology. He was previously President of a organization specializing in innovative educational and industrial applications of video technology.

DAVID HARKNESS (MBA) is Senior Vice President/Director of Marketing of the Nielsen Media Research Group, responsible for developing and marketing Nielsen's research services to the cable television industry and for special research on the new communications technologies.

JACK HILL was Vice President of Research for the Cable Television Advertising Bureau, responsible for the design of primary cable research and the analysis and interpretation of syndicated cable research data. He was previously an executive vice president for Simmons Market Research, and a senior vice president at Ogilvy and Mather.

DEAN M. KRUGMAN (Ph.D.) is Director of Graduate Studies and an Associate Professor of Advertising at the School of Journalism and Mass Communication, University of Georgia. His research focuses on advertising management and new communication technologies.

DONGHOON KIM is a Doctoral student at the Columbia Business School. His research interests include the estimation of brand equity from scanner panel data.

ROBERT MAXWELL (Ph.D.) is Vice President, Research, Home Box Office, Inc, responsible for all its research activities on programming and marketing operations. He previously worked as a manager of program research at ABC Entertainment.

DAVID POLTRACK (MBA) is Director of Marketing, CBS Inc., with whom he has been since 1969. He was previously with the Ted Bates advertising agency. Mr. Poltrack is the author of a book on television marketing, and is an adjunct Professor at New York University.

ROLAND T. RUST (Ph.D.) is Associate Professor and CBA Foundation Fellow at the University of Texas at Austin. His research focuses on advertising media models and marketing research methodology.

JONATHAN B. SIMS (MBA) is now Vice President of Research for the Cable Television Advertising Bureau. He has held a variety of media planning and research positions at General Foods, AGB Research, the Hearst Corporation, Foote Cone & Belding, and the Lever Brothers company.

SEYMOUR SUDMAN (Ph.D.) is Walter H. Stellner Distinguished Professor of Marketing and Professor of Business Administration and Sociology and Research Professor, Survey Research Laboratory, at the University of Illinois at Urbana-Champaign. Dr. Sudman is one of the world's leading experts on panels and other survey research methodologies, and has served as President of the American Association for Public Opinion Research.

W. WAYNE TALARZYK (Ph.D.) is Professor and Chairman of the Academic Faculty of Marketing at Ohio State University. His teaching and research interests lie primarily in the areas of consumer attitudes and lifestyles and new technologies in marketing, with a special emphasis on videotex. He is the author of several well-known college textbooks on consumer behavior.